COMBAT AIRCRAFT
155 Me 262 UNITS IN COMBAT

SERIES EDITOR TONY HOLMES

155

**COMBAT
AIRCRAFT**

Robert Forsyth

Me 262 UNITS IN COMBAT

OSPREY
PUBLISHING

OSPREY PUBLISHING

Bloomsbury Publishing Plc

Kemp House, Chawley Park, Cumnor Hill, Oxford OX2 9PH, UK

29 Earlsfort Terrace, Dublin 2, Ireland

1385 Broadway, 5th Floor, New York, NY 10018, USA

E-mail; info@ospreypublishing.com

www.ospreypublishing.com

OSPREY is a trademark of Osprey Publishing Ltd

First published in Great Britain in 2024

A catalogue record for this book is available from the British Library

ISBN: PB 9781472860774; eBook 9781472860781; ePDF 9781472860798;
XML 9781472860804

24 25 26 27 28 10 9 8 7 6 5 4 3 2 1

Edited by Tony Holmes
Cover Artwork by Gareth Hector
Aircraft Profiles by Jim Laurier
Index by Richard Munro
Typeset by PDQ Digital Media Solutions, UK
Printed by Repro India Ltd.

MIX
Paper
FSC FSC® C047271

Osprey Publishing supports the Woodland Trust, the UK's leading woodland
conservation charity.

To find out more about our authors and books visit **www.ospreypublishing.com**.
Here you will find extracts, author interviews, details of forthcoming events and
the option to sign up for our newsletter.

Acknowledgements

My thanks this time around to J Richard Smith, Eddie J Creek, Stephen Ransom,
Walter J Boyne, Nick Beale, Luigino Caliaro, Nick Stroud, Martin Streetly, Nevil
Basnett and Tony Holmes. Each time I revisit the Me 262, I am reminded of how
valuable my meetings and correspondence with the veterans of both sides were.
I would also like to thank the late Adolf Galland, Walter Krupinski, Erich
Hohagen, Eduard Schallmoser, Hermann Buchner, Herbert Schlüter, Walter
Windisch and John O Moench.

Front Cover

An Me 262A-1a/U3, depicted here as
'White 2' of 1./*Nahaufklärungsgruppe* 1
based at Zerbst, flies a typical solo
reconnaissance mission over the
countryside of Hessen, east of Frankfurt-
am-Main, intended to track advancing
American ground forces in early April 1945.
A small number of NAGr. 1's jets (around
seven in total) were ordered 'to cover the
central area as far west as Frankfurt/Main'
at this time, providing vital visual and photo-
reconnaissance on behalf of the high
commands of both the Luftwaffe and Heer
on the Western Front.

The Me 262A-1a/U3 was a modification
of the standard A-1a fighter variant, with
two Rb 50/30 cameras installed in the
nose, angled outwards at 11 degrees. The
aircraft portrayed in Gareth Hector's
artwork, Wk-Nr 500257, was built at
Regensburg and known to be in service
with NAGr. 1 by early April 1945. The
aircraft number, '2', is in the white of 1.
Staffel, while the nose is finished in black,
white and red segments, representing the
German national colours in a reference to
the circular insignia used on military caps
which was referred to on occasion as the
'Eye of Germany'. After a brief operational
period of about two weeks, 'White 2' was
destroyed by retreating Luftwaffe personnel
at Bernburg on 12 April

PREVIOUS PAGES

Me 262A-1a 'Black F', which was used by
Kdo. Schenck and I./KG 51, sits on a
compass swing table at Lechfeld in July
1944. The canopy was marked with two
diagonal targeting lines to assist a pilot in
making a dive-bombing attack. This aircraft
was fitted with a 'Wikingerschiff' ('Viking
Ship', so named after its shape) bomb rack
mounted on the underside of the fuselage
immediately aft of the nosewheel well,
offset to starboard, and which could carry
an SC 500 bomb (*EN Archive*)

CONTENTS

CHAPTER ONE

SPEED KINGS

I n certain respects, it is a wonder that the Messerschmitt Me 262 ever got airborne at all. It is a frequent irony that the more innovative an invention, the more that it can be restricted in its development and ultimate employment by lack of vision, technical understanding and/or funding, bureaucracy, disagreement and/or plain obstinacy. Such were the hindrances that faced global jet engine development in the 1920s and 1930s.

However, the principle of jet propulsion was not a new aeronautical breakthrough by those decades. Indeed, more than 2000 years earlier, around 400 BC, a Greek mathematician, astronomer and visionary named Archytas, who was a friend of Plato and a devotee of Pythagoras, is thought to have designed and constructed a wooden, bird-like machine that could fly by means of 'hidden and enclosed air'. Arguably, the air would probably have been vented, in which case Archytas may well have created the first form of 'jet propulsion' in a winged structure and, as aviation historian Richard P Hallion points out, this took place 'nearly two millennia in advance of the Italian Giovanni de Fontana's much better known 1420 illustration of a rocket-powered model bird'.

In July 1784, two bold French experimenters – Abbé Miolan and Janinet – attempted to fly a hot air balloon with a large hole in one side, believing that the 'jets' of hot air blowing out of the hole would propel the balloon in the opposite direction. They failed. With the balloon unable to fully inflate, a crowd of dissatisfied spectators decided to set fire to it.

The squat, bare-metal profile of the prototype Gloster-designed E.28/39 jet prior to it being painted in RAF camouflage. In Britain in the spring of 1941, this small aircraft, powered by Frank Whittle's turbojet, represented the future of aeronautical propulsion, although the sceptics then outnumbered the visionaries (*The Aviation Historian*)

Things were more considered by the 1920s, but there was still much scepticism when it came to the radical notion of 'propelling' an aeroplane without the means of a propeller. Jet propulsion was disregarded because it was considered to be inferior when set against the proven and tested piston engine, unless an aeroplane was able to fly at speeds of 650–800 km/h – which they could not. Of course, such a viewpoint failed to appreciate that jet propulsion as a means of power *could* make an aeroplane fly at such speeds.

In 1928 in England, Frank Whittle, a talented cadet at the RAF College at Cranwell, in Lincolnshire, who held a keen interest in engineering, wrote a paper entitled 'Future Developments in Aircraft Design' in which he prophesied that a new form of high-speed propulsion would be needed for aircraft as speed became an ever more necessary requirement. Whittle believed that speeds of 500 mph or greater would be achieved only at high altitudes where drag was minimised because of low air density, and piston engines were disadvantaged in thin air – a problem exacerbated by a whirling propeller.

Whittle came to recognise that a combination of the gas turbine (in which mechanical power is produced by hot combustion gases passing through a rotating turbine which then turns a shaft) with a piston engine could offer a powerful alternative. Experiments with gas turbines had proved disappointing, and to drive a propeller via a turbine was an inefficient prospect set against a standard piston engine. In combining the two types into a 'turbojet', air entered the front of an engine via a duct and was compressed mechanically, then used to burn injected liquid fuel which was expanded through a gas turbine to drive the compressor, with the hot gases ejected to provide 'jet' propulsion. A part of the energy in the exhaust gases formed in the jet's third stage turned the turbine, driving the compressor feeding the air in the first stage. Any loss in power due to the need to drive the turbine was countered by the store of energy in the gases available to generate thrust.

At higher altitudes this concept would offer efficient performance, with low air temperatures increasing thermal efficiency. Frank Whittle duly filed a patent for his concept on 6 January 1930, and it was granted 18 months later.

But Whittle's idea was met with apathy and the patent expired. In 1934, however, while at Cambridge to study engineering on behalf of the RAF, Whittle was able to devote further time to his designs. Encouraged by a professor, Whittle formed Power Jets Ltd in March 1936 in order to build an experimental model. He kept the design deliberately simple, and by April 1937 it was ready for testing. The engine performed satisfactorily, achieving running speeds of 12,000 rpm by the following month.

Then, at a dinner held by the Cambridge University Air Squadron, Whittle managed to secure the interest of the Air Ministry's Henry Tizard. Through Tizard's championship, a detailed report was prepared by the Air Ministry endorsing Whittle's work, although it was felt that jet propulsion was workable only for special requirements such as achieving high speed or attaining high altitude for brief periods.

It would not be until May 1939 that a contract was placed for an aircraft to be powered by Whittle's turbojet. With P E G Sayer at the controls, the

Gloster E.28/39 first took to the skies from Cranwell on 15 May 1941 powered by a Power Jets W.1 turbojet producing 860 lbs of thrust at 17,750 rpm.

In Italy, *Ingegnere* Secondo Campini had studied jet propulsion since 1929, and promoted his ideas in the aviation journal *L'Aeronautica* the following year. In 1931, he offered a proposal to the *Ministero dell'aeronautica* which differed from Whittle's design in as much as Campini proposed using a conventional reciprocating engine to drive a compressor before air was passed into a combustion chamber, where, mixed with fuel, it ignited. The proposal was rejected, but undaunted, Campini and his two brothers set about building an experimental boat powered by jet propulsion. The finished item was tested in Venice in April 1932, and although it reached an impressive speed of 28 knots, no further work on it ensued.

Two years later, Campini finally succeeded in securing an order for a test aircraft with which to prove his theories on the power of the aero jet engine. Campini's VENAR company teamed up with Società Italiana Caproni, and the project was shrouded in secrecy whilst work was carried out on two prototype airframes – the N.1 and N.2 – in a high-security building within Caproni's factory at Taliedo, near Milan. By 6 December 1936 the fuselage had been completed and, fitted with an 18-cylinder Isotta Fraschini Asso 750 R engine driving the compressor, the airframe underwent engine tests. These were disappointing, with thrust lower than the estimates. Nevertheless, Campini and Caproni secured further government funding, as well as an extension to the delivery deadline.

What eventually emerged as the N.1 (officially known as the C.2) was a low, elliptical wing aircraft with a long cylindrical fuselage comprising an air intake in the nose, the compressor, the centre section (which housed a radiator, the piston engine and afterburner equipment) and aft, in the tail section, the combustion chamber and the Pelton 'bullet' that controlled the 'jet' exit. Both the N.1 and N.2 were to be powered by 900 hp, 12-cylinder, liquid-cooled, Isotta Fraschini Asso XI L.121 RC40 reciprocating (piston) engines driving a three-stage ducted fan or compressor.

Flames streak from the 'motorjet' of the two-seat C.2 during a ground test probably at Milan-Taliedo or Milan-Linate in late 1940 or early 1941. In comparison to the diminutive E.28/29, the C.2 was much larger and heavier, and was underpowered. It is possible that Secondo Campini, the driving force behind the C.2, is sat in the aircraft's cockpit (*Luigino Caliaro*)

On 27 August 1940, N.2 flew for the first time, with 1926 Schneider Cup winner Colonnello Mario de Bernardi at the controls, although he did not initially light the afterburner when he flew the aircraft.

In its final form, the C.2 was an unarmed, two-seat aircraft 14.5 m in length and with a wing span of 12 m. It had a maximum speed of 328 km/h without afterburner and 375 km/h at 2987 m with it. With afterburner on, the C.2 could climb to 1000 m in around nine minutes.

However, despite flight testing continuing into the summer of 1942, the aircraft were dogged by performance issues, high fuel consumption, structural problems and leakages. A report prepared by the *Direzione Superiore degli Studi e delle Esperienze* at Guidonia, near Rome, concluded that, 'The trials have demonstrated the practical possibility of flight by other than normal airscrew propulsion, but, considering the very low speeds attained in the test flights, the advantages of jet propulsion are hardly shown in a favourable light'. No further such aircraft were built.

Yet both Italy and Britain were ahead of the US when it came to inter/ pre-war jet engine development. Indeed, it was not until April 1941 that Maj Gen Henry 'Hap' Arnold, Chief of the US Army Air Corps, visited Britain and witnessed the first flights of the new Gloster E.28/39. A man who recognised that, despite President Franklin D Roosevelt's call for 'lots' of aeroplanes, technology was a crucial factor in modern air power, Arnold quickly obtained British agreement to allow General Electric, a company which had experience with gas turbines, to take a serious look at Whittle's engine. However, although the subsequent Bell XP-59A Airacomet prototype twin-jet fighter took to the air powered by General Electric J31 engines within a year, no jet would see combat with the USAAF during World War 2.

Japan too would lag behind in the 'jet race', its Nakajima-built Kikka twin-engined jet fighter not taking to the air until 7 August 1945.

In Germany, however, since the late 1930s, aircraft designers and aeronautical engineers had been at work developing new technology in the form of the turbojet engine. Professor Georg Madelung, head of the Aerodynamics Institute at the Technical University in Stuttgart and a brother-in-law to the aircraft designer Willy Messerschmitt, put forward a proposal for a point defence fighter which used 'jet propulsion by means of extracting air for combustion and additional supercharged air masses from the atmosphere'.

But it had been the Heinkel company which had first got an aircraft powered by jet engines into the air. Design of what would become the diminutive, shoulder-winged He 178, commenced in early 1938 when the He 178 V1 flew for the first time on 27 August 1939 powered by a single 500 kp-thrust HeS 3b engine designed by Hans von Ohain. Further development resulted in the He 280, a design intended as a fighter which was powered in prototype form by twin Heinkel-built HeS (Heinkel *Strahltriebwerke* – 'Jet Engine') 8 engines which produced 700 kg of thrust.

The *Reichsluftfahrtministerium* (RLM – German Air Ministry) broadly supported the concept of a new generation of fighters powered by jet engines. However, the He 280, the world's first turbojet-powered fighter, was considered by the RLM to be too small and structurally

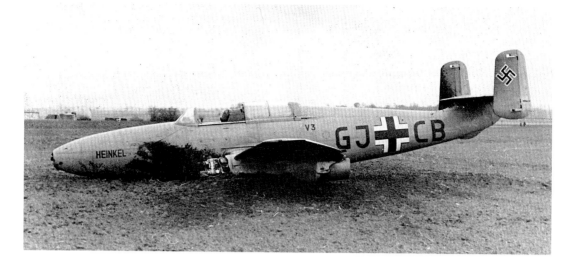

inadequate, paving the way for a larger, more promising design from Messerschmitt. In February 1940, Ernst Heinkel's contemporary, Professor Willy Messerschmitt, had enhanced the design of his P.1065 from the autumn of 1938 which led to an RLM specification dating from January 1939 calling for a high-speed interceptor, capable of a maximum speed of 900 km/h, to be powered by a single, unspecified jet engine.

Initially, the P.1065 featured a wing virtually identical in planform to the early Messerschmitt Bf 109 fighter, and it was to be powered by two BMW P.3304 turbojets that had been developed by Bramo and which were to be mounted centrally in the wings. Unfortunately, however, the planned engine, designated 109-002, was abandoned in 1942 after some major components had been built and tested statically. In February 1940, the P.1065 was modified to have its outer wing sections swept back 18 degrees 32 minutes in order to solve problems that the eventually larger engine diameters and heavier weight estimates for the P.3304 and P.3302 (109-003) caused with the positioning of the aircraft's centre of gravity.

In order to get the prototype P.1065 flying as soon as possible, it was proposed to fit it with a single 700 hp Junkers Jumo 210G piston engine in the nose, using a similar installation to that of the Bf 109D. As soon as they became available, two BMW P.3302 engines were to be mounted under the wings.

After wind tunnel-testing had shown that sweeping the wing back 18 degrees improved the aircraft's limiting Mach number, a proposal was issued on 4 April 1941 to develop a 35-degree swept-back wing under the designation *Pfeilflügel* ('arrow' or swept wing) I. This was to have an area of 20m² and a span of ten metres. Construction of the first P.1065 prototype took place in February–March 1941, the project receiving the official RLM designation 'Me 262' on 8 April. A few days previously, on 30 March, Heinkel's He 280 had made its first flight powered by two 720 kg-thrust HeS 8A turbojets.

An initial flight of the Me 262 V1 powered by two early BMW P.3302 turbojets on 25 March 1942 had to be terminated early when the port

The sleek form of the He 280 V3 prototype looking a little worse for wear on 8 February 1943 after a turbine blade broke away and pilot Fritz Schäfer had to land with the undercarriage up. By all accounts this aircraft flew again only three days later (*Wolfgang Mühlbauer*)

Fritz Wendel climbs from the cockpit of the Me 262 V3 PC+UC at Leipheim possibly in the spring of 1943 following its rebuild after sustaining damage on the ground with Heinrich Beauvais at the controls in August 1942. Note the Versuchs or prototype number applied to the tail assembly in white just forward of the Hakenkreuz (*EN Archive*)

turbojet malfunctioned at an altitude of 1000 m. The Me 262 finally took to the air for its first purely jet-powered flight on 18 July 1942 when company test pilot Fritz Wendel made a trouble-free flight in the third prototype (V3) from Leipheim.

BMW was still grappling with design issues, so the aircraft had been fitted with less complex Junkers Jumo 004A engines manufactured by the Junkers Flugzeug und Motorenwerke ('Jumo'). Work on these engines had begun in December 1939 under the day-to-day control of Dipl.-Ing. Anselm Franz. He favoured an axial system over centrifugal compressors and incorporated a single-stage turbine wheel, initially with solid blades along with a variable-area exhaust nozzle mounted in the engine's tailpipe, adjusted by using a servo-motor controlled by the throttle.

When Wendel flew the Me 262 with Jumo engines, he was able to report generally smooth handling whilst achieving an unprecedented airspeed of 720 km/h. Despite misgivings, Wendel also recorded that the engines 'worked well'. However, because of the large shadow looming over Messerschmitt as a result of major problems associated with the twin-piston-engined Me 210 fighter, the flight of the Me 262 had been low key, and according to the company's commercial director, Rakan Kokothaki, it went 'completely unobserved'.

Nevertheless, to the RLM, there were clear attractions and advantages in the jet engine. The Jumo 004, at least, was lighter than an equivalent piston engine, with a high power-to-weight ratio. Furthermore, its smaller profile and lack of a propeller assisted in reducing drag – an important factor for a fighter. However, in 1939, as the prospect of war darkened the skies over Europe, investment in terms of money, time, personnel and industrial resources in 'fanciful', experimental and risky forms of technology were shelved. Thus, when it came to military aviation, that meant favouring established designs which resulted in the minimum of disruption to assembly lines and the unnecessary diversion of resources down 'blind alleys'. During World War 2, almost all the main designs of fighter, bomber, reconnaissance, maritime and ground-attack aircraft were either pre-war in origin or types based on improvement rather than innovation.

American historian Stephen Budiansky opines that, 'Were it not for the war, the jet airplane might actually have gotten off the ground sooner. No one was about to gamble the war effort on an unproven idea'. By mid-1944 in Nazi Germany, however, it was no longer a gamble, but rather an increasingly desperate faith and hope that in the jet engine there was the means that could prevent impending defeat.

CHAPTER TWO

A DUBIOUS DEBUT

When Messerschmitt's new jet interceptor – the recently named Me 262 V1 – rolled out of the assembly hall at Augsburg during the evening of 18 April 1941 for its first flight, the aircraft had no jets. Rather, it was powered by a single, nose-mounted 700 hp Jumo 210G piston engine driving a two-bladed propeller and lacked the nosewheel that would become a main feature in years to come. The wing design was also at an evolutionary stage and did not incorporate the straighter, more refined swept-back leading edge that would appear on eventual production models. As if to emphasise its somewhat unready state, the V1 had also been fitted with the rudder from the second prototype, the V2.

At the controls was Messerschmitt test pilot Flugkapitän Fritz Wendel, a blunt man who did not spare from expressing his opinions. The day before, he had carried out a successful ground test on the aircraft. Now, carrying 150 litres of fuel and 35 litres of oil, the V1 weighed 3080 kg. After the first flight, which went off satisfactorily, Wendel reported;

'At the present centre of gravity, the vertical stabiliser is set at +1°. After taxiing for 600–700m, the machine is able to lift off. The slats open perfectly, except for a slight difference in the times of opening between the left and right sides. Take-off speed is 170 km/h. Landing flaps are extended to 25° for take-off.'

Fitted with the same engine, the Me 262 V1 achieved a maximum speed of 420 km/h in level flight and 540 km/h in a dive from 7000m in

The shark-like elegance of the Me 262 emerges in this photograph of V5 prototype PC+UE. This was the first machine to be fitted with a nosewheel based on the piston-engined Me 309, an aircraft which never advanced beyond the experimental stage. The V5, which had a fixed undercarriage, flew for the first time on 6 June 1943. The new 'tricycle' arrangement provided improved forward vision for the pilot. Note the prototype number applied to the tail fin and the protective grilles fitted over the engine intakes (*EN Archive*) subsequent flight tests. Not a lot happened after that, although pilots from the Luftwaffe's main test centre at Rechlin did fly the aircraft on 4 August. Four days later, the Luftwaffe's head of procurement, Generaloberst Ernst Udet, was shown a prototype that demonstrated the future in as much as it had been fitted with mock-up jet units. So far, so good.

The test progamme, combined with further development, continued, but it would not be until the following year that the V1 would make its first jet-powered flight from Augsburg, and even then it was a disappointing event. The aircraft appeared with a somewhat incongruous configuration, fitted as it was with its nose piston engine and two wing-mounted, provisional BMW prototype turbojets.

After a five-hour delay while final preparations were made, during the evening of 25 March 1942, Wendel – in the cockpit once again – waited as the turbojets ran up and then began to taxi out. But the pilot was too heavy on the throttles and both jet engines cut out. They were restarted, and the aircraft eventually took off at 1929 hrs. Wendel noted that he needed 800–900 m of runway to lift off, after which he climbed for 20 seconds and then levelled out as airspeed increased to around 450 km/h. The problems did not end there, however, for Wendel – a very experienced pilot – struggled to master handling the turbojets. He quickly returned to earth, managing to land normally, although the aircraft's shock absorbers broke in the process. In his subsequent report, Wendel stated that an 'average pilot' would be unable to control the Me 262 in its present state.

By the following July the third prototype (V3) had been fitted with Jumo 004A-0 (T1) turbojets – units which, less complex in design and construction than BMW engines, offered more promise. Wendel flew the Me 262 V3 twice from Leipheim with the Jumos fitted on 18 July, the first

Flugkapitän Fritz Wendel, a world airspeed record-breaking Messerschmitt test pilot, flew the Me 262 prototypes on several occasions, and also toured the initial Luftwaffe units which operated the type. Wendel did not spare his criticism of the jet's early shortcomings or of the operational units, particularly *Kdo. Nowotny*, but was objective in his detailed reports to Messerschmitt (*EN Archive*)

time that the aircraft would fly in the configuration for which it would become known operationally, although at this stage it was still a 'taildragger'. Things went satisfactorily, and despite the delayed gestation of both aircraft and powerplant, Wendel was able to report generally smooth handling of the Me 262 during the maiden test-flight, in which he achieved an unprecedented airspeed of 720 km/h. Regardless of any misgivings he may have harboured, Wendel also recorded that the Junkers T1 engines 'worked well'.

Heinrich Beauvais, a fighter specialist from Rechlin, arrived at Leipheim on 11 August to test the V3 for the RLM. Wendel briefed him on how to raise the tail during take-off, but the latter failed to achieve sufficient speed and careered off the runway into a field. Ignobly, the aircraft's starboard wing cut into a dung heap. It spun around and both mainwheel supports and engines were torn off in the process. All further flight-testing on the Me 262 was forced to stop for six weeks since there was a lack of engines for the V1 and the V2. On 1 October, the latter prototype flew successfully with Jumo units from Lechfeld, where the runway was longer than at Leipheim.

The following day, the RLM increased its existing order for pre-production aircraft to 30. From then on, until mid-1944, development of the Me 262 pressed ahead using a series of prototypes to test all aspects of the aircraft. At Lechfeld in May 1943, the *General der Jagdflieger*, Generalmajor Adolf Galland, flew the V4 prototype and recognised in it an aircraft with which Germany could capture the initiative in the air war over Europe, especially since the prospect of higher-performance Allied fighters in increasing numbers was very real, along with an ever-expanding USAAF heavy bomber force. He famously commented to observers on the ground after his flight that, 'It felt as if angels were pushing!' Four months later, the V1 and V3, active once more in the test programme, undertook tests to assess slat operation, spin characteristics and high-speed performance. The V3 reached 950 km/h during tests in October.

With the advance technology of its engines and the resulting high speed, as well as the inherent combat capability and quality of its airframe, Galland became seduced by the potential of the Me 262. He championed its rapid development and wrote enthusiastically to his superiors in the RLM that all measures should be taken to ensure swift and large-scale production. Despite lingering problems associated with take-off and landing, fuel feed and stability, in a report to Generalfeldmarschall Erhard Milch, the *Generalluftzeugmeister*, Galland wrote;

'The aircraft represents a great step forward and could be our greatest chance; it could guarantee us an unimaginable lead over the enemy if he adheres to the piston engine.'

He pushed for the cancellation of the piston-engined Me 209 project, which was intended as the replacement of the Bf 109 fighter, in favour of the jet interceptor. In April 1943 Hauptmann Wolfgang Späte, a Knight's Cross-holder and then 72-victory fighter ace, had flown the V2 and reported to Galland that;

'The climbing speed of the Me 262 surpasses that of the Bf 109G by 5 to 6 m/sec. The superior horizontal and climbing speeds will enable the aircraft to operate successfully against numerically superior enemy fighters. The extremely heavy armament (six [sic] 30 mm guns) permits attacks on bombers at high approach speeds with destructive results, despite the short time the aircraft is in the firing position.'

The following month, in a meeting held at the RLM, Oberstleutnant Edgar Petersen, the overall chief of the Luftwaffe's test centres, told Milch that Späte had 'a lot of experience on the [Me] 163 and is 300 per cent more in favour of the [Me] 262'.

That may have been the case, but low points were encountered when some of the early prototypes crashed and one test pilot lost his life – on 18 April, Oberfeldwebel Wilhelm Ostertag was killed when one of the Jumo 004s fitted to the V2 (the very aircraft that Späte had flown) flamed out, throwing the machine into a steep dive from which it never recovered. But Milch became

Me 262 S1 VI+AF undergoes gun calibration on a firing range possibly at Augsburg (its place of manufacture) or Lechfeld. Note the removed nosecone and access panels covering the MK 108 cannon installation. The first of the *'Serienflugzeuge'*, this aircraft did not enjoy an illustrious career, with a list of 66 problem items being drawn up in connection with its build quality shortly after the jet was completed. It is believed to have flown for the first time on 19 April 1944, and despite various technical faults and accidents, the S1 soldiered on for at least another two months, but its fate is not certain (*EN Archive*)

encouraged by Galland's enthusiasm and gave priority to the Me 262 building programme.

Unfortunately, an American air raid on the Regensburg assembly plant in August 1943 destroyed crucial fuselage jigs and acceptance gauges and forced Messerschmitt to relocate its project office from Augsburg to Oberammergau, in the Bavarian Alps. Also, the promised 1800 skilled workers needed to tool-up production lines arrived late, resulting in the loss of almost three-million man hours in nine months. During a discussion concerning labour requirements at a conference held at the Armaments Ministry on 19 January 1944, Milch commented to ministry adviser Major Dr Krome, 'We need the Me 262 more than anything else – more than submarines, more than tanks, because without this aircraft all armament production will become impossible'.

Clearly, Milch knew that the Luftwaffe needed an efficient, fast, manoeuvrable and yet heavily armed interceptor to deal with the increasing threat posed by the USAAF's formations of heavily armed and escorted bombers targeting the Reich's key centres of production. Indeed, with a view to tackling this threat, as early as the spring of 1943, he had investigated the possibility of developing a more heavily armoured variant known as the *Panzerflugzeug*, but the adverse effect of the additional weight compromised range.

The Me 262 programme suffered a further loss of life on 9 March 1944 when Feldwebel Kurt Schmidt was killed in the Me 262 V6 following a crash, although flight-testing continued with four more prototypes – V7–V10 – all committed and all featuring the new nosewheel as part of a tricycle undercarriage design. Additionally, a short run of series aircraft was under construction at Leipheim, these initial machines being designated 'S' for *Serien*. With the exception of the S2 and the S10, which were used by Messerschmitt for assessment, the initial batch of aircraft (S1–S22) was slated for the Luftwaffe, although several machines were destroyed in USAAF bombing raids – ironically, the exact scenario which Milch feared.

Aside from American bombs, however, another difficulty which dogged development and delivery of the Me 262 was the ongoing lack of Jumo 004 engines. On 25 April Professor Messerschmitt wrote to the production director of the Jumo engine plant at Dessau imploring him to overcome problems and delays associated with delivery of the badly needed turbojets. 'It is a matter of life and death for us all to set up the numbers of Me 262s with your engines as rapidly as possible.' Given these adversities, it is impressive that the first operational variant, the Me 262A-1a, an interceptor based on entirely new concepts in aeronautical design and technology, reached the Luftwaffe within three months of Messerschmitt's letter.

Erprobungskommando 262

It is believed that the first tentative step taken by Messerschmitt directed at the Luftwaffe's employment of the Me 262 was the establishment, in late 1943, of the innocuously named *Autobedarf Lechfeld* (*Autobedarf* – 'Motor supplies'). This was a cover name used for a small unit from the company's flight-testing department that set itself up on the western edge of Lechfeld airfield, 20 km south of Augsburg.

Lechfeld was an important airfield established in 1935, and by late 1943 it had a single, paved, camouflaged and illuminated runway of approximately 1965 x 50 m supporting an infrastructure of one medium and five large hangars, paved aprons, extensive workshops, control and administration buildings, accommodation and an officers' mess, all protected by three light Flak positions on the airfield

Eight new Me 262A-1as of *E.Kdo* 262 lined up at Lechfeld in the summer of 1944. The aircraft in the foreground, Wk-Nr 170071 'White 2', not only survived the war, it was distinctive at the time of this photograph for having only two gun ports but four ammunition ejection chutes. In October 1944 the aircraft was reported as having deformed wing surfaces and bent mainwheel doors, but it was later assigned to III./EJG 2 and was flown by Knight's Cross recipients Major Erich Hohagen and Oberfeldwebel Hermann Buchner. Wk-Nr 170067 'White 3' immediately next to it was another survivor, ending the war on the strength of I./KG(J) 54. Note the lesser seen white Hakenkreuz on Wk-Nr 170045 'White 5' immediately behind 'White 3' (*EN Archive*)

perimeter. Lechfeld had a dual function, serving as an *Industriehafen* (factory airfield) for final assembly and testing for the Messerschmitt company, as well as a main Luftwaffe base where day and nightfighter and bomber training was undertaken. For example, conversion training was carried out here for crews destined to fly the Me 410 and He 177.

The *Autobedarf Lechfeld* was coordinated by the head of Messerschmitt flight-testing, Dipl.-Ing. Gerhard Caroli, and he would liaise with the Luftwaffe as it set about establishing the first Me 262 operational testing unit at Lechfeld, to be known as *Erprobungskommando* (*E.Kdo*) 262. On paper at least, the *Kommando* is believed to have become a formal entity on, or by, 9 December 1943. Six days after that, the unit was assigned a commanding officer in the shape of Hauptmann Werner Thierfelder.

Thierfelder, who as a boy had grown up in South West Africa (now Namibia), was a veteran combat pilot and was selected for his role because of his twin-engined fighter experience flying Bf 110s with *Zerstörergeschwader* (ZG) 26 and ZG 2, as well for as his technical acumen, which would be valuable when it came to understanding the idiosyncrasies of the new jet engine. Having seen service over France, England, the Balkans and Crete, he had been awarded the Knight's Cross on 10 October 1941. By the time he took command of *E.Kdo* 262, he had accounted for 27 enemy aircraft destroyed in the air and 41 on the ground.

On 21 December Thierfelder made his first flight in an Me 262 when he piloted the V6 over Lechfeld. Also invited to fly the machine that day for an assessment was Major Egon Mayer, the *Kommodore* of *Jagdgeschwader* (JG) 2. Like Thierfelder, Mayer was an accomplished fighter ace and tactician, especially when it came to fighting four-engined bombers, and so his opinion mattered. As far as is known, neither man had any concerns about the jet interceptor. Nevertheless, progress with *E.Kdo* 262 was grindingly slow. It was not until 20 January 1944 that Thierfelder was assigned his first three pilots, Feldwebel Helmut Baudach and Feldwebel Erwin Eichhorn from JG 2, while Feldwebel Helmut Lennartz was posted in from 5./JG 11, where he had flown mortar-equipped Bf 109s against American bombers.

At the end of February, a fourth pilot joined when Oberleutnant Ernst Wörner came from his position as *Staffelkapitän* of 2./ZG 101, where he had instructed on the twin-engined Bf 110 – another man who would, hopefully, prove useful when it came to the Me 262. In May 1941 Wörner had been one of the small group of Luftwaffe aircrew to fly Bf 110s with *Sonderkommando Junck* in Iraq. He was a recipient of the *Deutsches Kreuz* in Gold.

Aircraft were also slow in coming, but in early 1944, flights were still very much concerned with familiarisation rather than any operational training. Thierfelder was able to test the already repaired V5, but on 1 February its nosewheel failed on landing at Lechfeld and the ensuing crash resulted in it being written off, although Thierfelder was unhurt. The *Kommando* was unable to resume testing until the V8 became available, and in which Lennartz flew on 19 April, and then in mid-May the S3 and S4 were also delivered. The S3 was flown on at least three occasions by Oberleutnant Ernst Tesch, a former reconnaissance pilot and instructor, but on all flights he experienced either mechanical or handling problems, while Lennartz, who also piloted it, experienced control issues. The S4 suffered tyre damage on two occasions attributed to anti-aircraft shell fragments on the runway at Lechfeld.

At last, in early May, a cadre of more pilots arrived. III./ZG 26 had been flying Bf 110 *Zerstörer* against USAAF bomber formations during the attacks on German aircraft manufacturing centres in February. On the 20th of that month the *Gruppe* had lost 11 of 13 aircraft deployed. Severely battered from such attritional missions, III./ZG 26 would convert to the Me 410 in March, but in the interim several of its pilots were reposted to *E.Kdo 262* while groundcrew were despatched to either Leipheim or Schwäbisch-Hall for technical instruction on the Me 262.

Among the pilots were the *Staffelkapitän* of 8./ZG 26, Oberleutnant Hans-Günther Müller, and the commander of 9./ZG 26, Oberleutnant Paul Bley. The reality, however, was that Müller and Bley effectively became ferry pilots, as there was little for them to do except pick up those few aircraft from Leipheim and Schwäbisch Hall that were assigned to the *Kommando*. Two other pilots from *E.Kdo 262*, Feldwebel Franz Herlitzius and Unteroffizier Hans Flachs, were eventually seconded to Messerschmitt's flight-test department, while others returned to ZG 26.

Throughout the summer of 1944, despite being plagued by poor build standards and faulty parts in the eight or so aircraft that it did have, *E.Kdo 262* endeavoured to implement some kind of familiarisation and training regime at Lechfeld with its limited number of jets and handful of pilots. This meant that the prospect of devising tactics was, realistically, some way off in the future.

There was a blow on 18 July when Thierfelder was killed flying the Me 262 S6. In what may have been one of the earliest attempts at combat deployment of the aircraft, he had taken off, necessarily, to engage enemy bombers which had approached Kaufering, dangerously near to Lechfeld. Although the bombers were escorted by P-51s, it is believed the S6 may have suffered some kind of engine malfunction. Although Thierfelder bailed out, he was too low for his parachute to open. The aircraft crashed into a field near Buchloe and was destroyed.

By late July, the unit was operating some of the first production variants. In its standard form the Me 262A-1a was an elegant, low-wing, all-metal, twin-jet, single-seat interceptor with 18.5-degree swept-back wings bearing a span of 12.56 m, a shark-like fuselage 10.6 m in length incorporating a nosewheel, and a large, high, tail assembly to which were fitted horizontal stabilisers also with swept-back leading edges. The equipped weight, allowing for a pilot, ammunition and a fuel load of just over 1800 litres was 6074 kg. The pilot was accommodated in a self-contained sub-assembly which held the instrument panel, electrical controls, control column, throttles, seat and battery. This *'Wanne'* (tub) was designed to break free on impact in the case of a crash-landing, offering the pilot some degree of enclosed protection. The cockpit was capped by a hinged, all-round-vision, canopy.

As an interceptor, the Me 262 was armed with four 30 mm Rheinmetall-Borsig MK 108 cannon mounted in the nose with a total of 360 rounds. The twin Jumo 004 engines were each 3.8 m long and weighed between 730-750 kg. These ground-breaking, state-of-the-art powerplants gave the Me 262 a climbing speed of 10 m/sec at 6000 m (allowing it to attain this altitude from take-off in seven minutes) and 5.2 m/sec at 9000 m (taking 14 minutes to reach this altitude from take-off). Maximum range at 6000 m was 520 km, and more than 644 km at 9000 m.

Encounters with Allied aircraft were sporadic and results were uncertain. On 25 July, Leutnant Alfred Schreiber, a former Bf 110 pilot with ZG 101 and ZG 26, had a brush with a Mosquito PR XVI over southern Germany and Austria. Schreiber wrongly claimed the Mosquito shot down, but in a series of evasive turns, and seeking the sanctuary of cloud, the Allied aircraft had managed to evade the jet. Nevertheless, in a double-edged assessment, British Intelligence later noted that;

'At times it appeared that the high speed of the enemy aircraft was a disadvantage in that it rapidly overshot when coming up from astern and had to make a wide turn in order to retrieve its position. The fact that it could make a wide turn, travelling in the opposite direction of the Mosquito to do so, and still get into position again gives some idea of its superior speed.'

Schreiber claimed a Spitfire for the *Kommando*'s second victory on 2 August, but this has not been substantiated, and six days later Leutnant Joachim Weber is believed to have shot down a Mosquito of the USAAF's 802nd Reconnaissance Group. In the afternoon of the 18th, Flt Lt F L Dodd, flying a Mosquito PR XVI of No 544 Sqn, encountered an Me 262 of *E.Kdo* 262 over Giebelstadt just after he had completed his reconnaissance of the area. The jet came in head-on, but Dodd quickly dived from 30,000 ft to 20,000 ft and the enemy interceptor was not seen again. Although relatively few and far between, these initial spars gave the Allies a wake-up call to the effect that the Luftwaffe had a new and potentially potent high-speed fighter.

On 5 August, following the loss of Thierfelder, Hauptmann Horst Geyer, former head of the weapons testing unit *E.Kdo* 25, took command of *E.Kdo* 262. Geyer oversaw the unit's operations until October, by which time it had claimed a handful of Allied aircraft shot down – mainly long-range reconnaissance Mosquitos and Spitfires – over southern Germany. Following his claim for a USAAF F-5 Lightning on 24 August, Oberfeldwebel Helmut Baudach received a letter from no less than Professor Willy Messerschmitt, in which the aircraft designer enthused;

'I congratulate you on this great success, which for me means the joy of knowing that our latest design has been proven and gives us the certainty that air supremacy can be regained over our homeland.'

AN UNPROMISING START

By late August 1944, Galland recognised that if the Me 262 was to be employed by the Luftwaffe in any numbers, and thus with any effectiveness, an expanded training environment was urgently needed. To this end he proposed the establishment of three specialist *Einsatzkommandos* to be set up at Lechfeld, Rechlin-Lärz and Erfurt-Bindersleben. Apart from continuing to address ongoing technical issues, their other main function would be to devise a tactical plan for deployment which could be adopted by any future Me 262 *Staffeln* or *Gruppen* that might be formed. This would be in addition to those personnel of III./ZG 26 which had been seconded for training to Messerschmitt with a view to being sent on to *E.Kdo* 262.

Surprisingly, it was intended that the new *Kommandos* would provide preliminary flying training as well as operational training, all of which would be conducted using twin-engined types such as the Si 204, Bf 110, the questionable Me 210 and even the Ta 154, alongside the Me 262 itself for advanced operational training.

In theory, Hauptmann Geyer was to retain overall command of the new Me 262 units, but to accelerate tactical development, Galland brought in Major Walter Nowotny. An Austrian recipient of the highest award to the Knight's Cross, the Diamonds, he had been credited with 255 victories while flying with I./JG 54 in the Soviet Union, although more recently he had been 'resting' in southwestern France in command of the fighter training unit JG 101.

By the end of August the *Kommandos* at Lechfeld and Lärz were operational, while the third was to be placed under the command of Oberleutnant Günther Wegmann, who had joined *E.Kdo* 262 from *Stab* III./ ZG 26. Following a hurried assessment, from the available personnel that the *Kommandos* absorbed, it was quickly recognised that only around 15 pilots were sufficiently competent to fly the jet interceptor operationally.

Meanwhile, flying from Lechfeld on 5 September, Leutnant Schreiber of *E.Kdo* 262 shot down a Spitfire PR XI of the USAAF's 7th Photographic Reconnaissance Group (PRG) on a mission to obtain bomb damage assessment imagery of Stuttgart, Ludwigshafen and Karlsruhe. Over Stuttgart, Schreiber approached the Spitfire flown by 2Lt Robert B. Hillborn of the 14th Photographic Reconnaissance Squadron from below, firing bursts from his MK 108, and then streaked past above it. The engine of Hillborn's aircraft promptly seized up and the bewildered pilot was forced to bail out.

Major Walter Nowotny (left), one of the Luftwaffe's star fighter aces, shares a lighter moment with Willi Kaether (centre), a technical director with Focke-Wulf, and Professor Kurt Tank (in fur-collared jacket) during a visit to the Focke-Wulf factory at Langenhagen in December 1943. Whilst there, among other things, Nowotny would inspect the Ta 154 nightfighter. A few months later, he was appointed commander of a new Me 262 interceptor operational evaluation unit, but his assignment proved challenging and would lead, ultimately, to his death (*EN Archive*)

While the new *Einsatzkommandos* formed up, *E.Kdo* 262 continued to make occasional engagements against enemy incursions. The day after Schreiber's aerial victory, Oberfeldwebel Hubert Göbel shot down a Mosquito, and on the 11th, Oberfeldwebel Baudach accounted for a P-51 Mustang of the 339th Fighter Group (FG), which crashed near Eberbach, its pilot forced to bail out. Leutnant Weber struck twice, on the 14th and the 18th, claiming a Mosquito on each day for his second and third victories while flying the Me 262.

At the beginning of October, the *Einsatzkommandos* and elements of *E.Kdo* 262 were formed into a new unit known as *Kommando* (*Kdo.*) *Nowotny* after its commander, and comprising three *Staffeln* with a nominal strength of 16 aircraft each. 1./*Kdo. Nowotny* was led by Oberleutnant Bley, 2. *Staffel* by Knight's Cross-holder Oberleutnant Alfred Teumer, who would have been known to Nowotny from his extensive service with JG 54, and 3. *Staffel* by veteran fighter pilot Hauptmann Georg- Peter Eder, who had flown with 4./JG 51, III./JG 2, II./JG 1 and II./JG 26. Also a recipient of the Knight's Cross, Eder, while *Staffelkapitän* of 12./JG 2 in late 1942, had been instrumental in working with Hauptmann Egon Mayer to develop the principle of the head on attack against four engined bombers.

Despite such talent heading the ranks of the new unit, no one could take the Me 262 for granted. This was proven on 4 October when, shortly after having taken off from Braunschweig en route to the newly designated base at Hesepe, Oberleutnant Teumer radioed control that he was experiencing problems with his starboard engine and throttle. His Me 262A-1a made it to Hesepe but the engine failed on arrival, the aircraft crashed and Teumer was killed. By this stage of the war, Teumer's loss was another the Luftwaffe fighter arm could ill afford – he had flown 300 missions and been credited with 76 victories, including ten in the West.

Teumer's place as *Kapitän* of 2./*Kdo. Nowotny* was taken by Leutnant Franz Schall, another Eastern Front ace who, in August 1944, had purportedly claimed 13 victories in one day while with I./JG 52. But the very day that Teumer was lost, Schall had a lucky escape when his jet crashed on landing at Waggum following a technical fault.

Kdo. Nowotny attempted to fly its first operational sortie 'in force' on 7 October against one of the largest American daylight bombing raids so far

An Opel Blitz fuel bowser and trailer pulls up in front of a line-up of Me 262A-1as of *Kdo. Nowotny* at Achmer in the autumn of 1944. The *Kommando's* aircraft were recognisable by their boldly mottled tail fins, white code numbers and yellow fuselage bands (*EN Archive*)

Leutnant Franz Schall poses for a photograph with a member of his groundcrew in front of Me 262 'White 1'. He joined *Kdo. Nowotny* in the autumn of 1944 and went on to command 10./JG 7. Awarded the Knight's Cross in October 1944, Schall is credited with 133 victories claimed during some 550 missions (*EN Archive*)

mounted, aimed at oil targets in central Germany. Taking off from Hesepe, Schall and Lennartz each claimed a B-24 shot down, thus giving the unit its first victories. However, it would be a different story for the *Staffel* freshly based at Achmer. As Bley, Leutnant Gerhard Kobert and Oberfähnrich Heinz Russel prepared to take off, a P-51 of the 361st FG flown by 1Lt Urban L Drew dived down from 5000 m, strafing the Me 262s lining up for take-off. Russel's aircraft collapsed, Kobert's blew up and Bley's was just airborne but then crashed, although he was able to bail out.

Isolated victories against Mustangs on 10 and 12 October did little to counter the opinions of Fritz Wendel, who visited *Kdo. Nowotny* as part of a Messerschmitt technical field team;

'*Kommando Nowotny* has been in action since 3 October 1944. Up until 24 October sorties had been flown on a total of three days. The Inspector of the Day Fighters, Oberst [Hannes] Trautloft, was at the base during the first days, and had made great personal efforts to ensure the success of the first fighter sorties with the Me 262. He saw to it that several successful fighter pilots were taken from other units to form the core of this unit. The commander, Major Nowotny, is a successful Eastern Front pilot, but is unfamiliar with the present situation in the West and, at 23, is not the superior leader personality necessary to guarantee the success of this vital operation.'

Wendel went on to criticise the unit's lack of coherent objective, pointing out contradictory opinions among its personnel;

'Instruction on the aircraft type is particularly bad with *Kommando Nowotny*. The importance given to the technical side may be illustrated by the fact that the *Gruppe* Technical Officer at Achmer, Hptm Streicher, is not a technician. The *Staffel* Technical Officer at Hesepe, 19-year-old Oberfähnrich Russel, is also a complete layman, who has himself recently destroyed two aircraft as a result of carelessness and inadequate training.'

As if this was not damning enough, circumstances were now playing into the hands of those who saw a very different role for the jet – that of a high-speed bomber. In his April 1943 report, even Hauptmann Wolfgang Späte had observed 'as a fighter-bomber, and carrying bombs, the aircraft would still be faster than any enemy fighter'.

Kdo. Nowotny struggled on into November. Oberfähnrich Willi Banzhaff of 3. *Staffel* was forced to bail out following an encounter with P-51s over Holland on the first day of the month, while on the 2nd there was some cheer when a P-51 and a P-47 were shot down by Feldwebel Erich Büttner and a P-47 by Oberfeldwebel Baudach. However, these events were tempered by the loss of Unteroffizier Alois Zollner, who was killed when his Me 262 crashed on take-off from Achmer. Another three jets were lost on 4 November in action against Mustangs. On the 6th, four more

Me 262s from the *Kommando* were damaged, three of them in emergency landings apparently as a result of fuel shortage. The solitary success for the unit that day came when Leutnant Schall destroyed a P-47.

Galland, already concerned at the increasing losses being suffered by his only jet fighter unit, arrived at Achmer on 7 November for an inspection. The next day, as the USAAF bombed the Nordhorn Canal and the marshalling yards at Rheine, the *Kommando* was able to despatch just four jets in two missions against the bombers. There was an inauspicious beginning when Nowotny found that he was unable to start his aircraft for the first mission in the morning, while another machine suffered a burst tyre. In the second mission, that afternoon, Nowotny finally took off to engage the enemy. During his subsequent encounter, he shot down a four-engined bomber and a P-51, but as he returned home he was apparently intercepted by an American fighter. A short while later, Nowotny's crackling voice was heard over the radio.

'We stepped into the open', Galland later wrote. 'Visibility was not good – six-tenths cloud. Seconds later, an Me 262 appeared out of the cloud and dived vertically into the ground. There was black smoke and an explosion'. Nowotny's last words, though garbled, indicated that his aircraft was hit and on fire, and seconds later he crashed to his death.

The death of Major Walter Nowotny effectively marked the end of the *Kommando* that bore his name, and it had not been a particularly glorious chapter in the history of the Me 262. Of around 30 Me 262s delivered to the unit, 26 are known to have been lost for one reason or another, the greater part through combat or indirectly as a result of combat or, equally worryingly, because of take-off or landing accidents and malfunctions. However, Nowotny's name, together with the aircraft which his unit had flown, would re-emerge as the honour title adopted by a much larger, more structured interceptor unit over the forthcoming weeks.

An Me 262 of *E.Kdo* 262 or III./EJG 2 about to take on J2 fuel from an Opel Blitz bowser. Used by the Jumo 004 jet engine, J2 was of lower grade than the B3 spirit need to run piston-engined fighters. As the war entered its final months, supply to Luftwaffe units was often interrupted. Note the protective wire grille positioned over the engine intake (*EN Archive*)

CHAPTER THREE

VIRTUES OF NECESSITY

A mechanic driving a *Kettenkrad* glances over his shoulder as he checks the cable connected to the mainwheels of an Me 262A-2a of I./KG 51 at Rheine in the early autumn of 1944. The aircraft carry the distinctive wavy camouflage typically seen on the *Geschwader*'s jets, as well as white nose tips and gun ports denoting 1. *Staffel* (*EN Archive*)

A s the pilots of *Kdo. Nowotny* attempted to master their impressive but daunting new jet interceptor, an initiative to deploy the aircraft in a very different way was at an advanced stage.

On 10 November 1944, just two days after Nowotny's death, around 50 km away from Achmer to the southwest, at Rheine, a formation of four Me 262s took off and headed westwards towards the Nijmegen road and rail bridge spanning the River Waal – a key objective for the Allied armies as they advanced eastwards. The dreary autumn weather on the Western Front had improved by the 10th, and British, Canadian, Polish and US forces had successfully cleared the area south of the River Maas of German resistance as they drove towards the Rhine.

The Me 262s that took off from Rheine belonged to I. *Gruppe* of *Kampfgeschwader* (KG) 51, and each jet carried two SD 250 anti-personnel bomb containers. This veteran bomber *Gruppe*, led by Hauptmann Heinz Unrau, had converted from the twin-engined Me 410 fast bomber in May 1944, and since late August had been carrying out high-speed bombing attacks against Allied troop and motorised columns and nodal road targets on the Western Front using the Me 262. In reality, these were little more than nuisance missions given the number of operational jets the *Gruppe* could draw upon at any one time.

One of the I./KG 51 pilots, Leutnant Heinrich Haeffner, experienced problems with his undercarriage soon after take-off and fell behind, but the remaining three jets made it to the target. They then encountered three Spitfires, and were prevented from carrying out their mission. Haeffner flew on alone through low-lying cloud and dropped both of his bombs on the bridge while under intense anti-aircraft (AA) fire. Results were not observed, and the mission does not seem to have hindered the Allied advance in any way. It was typical of the kind of operation that the *Gruppe* was undertaking at this time, but for the Allies, such raids were little more than occasional pinpricks.

Despite surviving German records, and the post-war viewpoints of a small number of senior figures involved in the process, the circumstances that led to the emergence of the Me 262 as a bomber remain shrouded in uncertainty, confusion and contradiction. Indeed, surviving RLM records paint a picture of confusion generated largely by industrial failings, distrust and competing interests. However a few facts have been ascertained as best they can.

In February 1943, the *Führer*, Adolf Hitler, ordered that *all* Luftwaffe fighters should be capable of carrying bombs so as to operate as fighter-bombers. To satisfy Hitler's requirements, in the summer of 1943, Messerschmitt designers worked on a range of developments for the Me 262, extending the aircraft's role as an interceptor to that of fighter-bomber, high-speed bomber and reconnaissance aircraft. The concept of a high-speed bomber ('*Schnellbomber I*') proposed a design similar in shape to the standard Me 262A-1a fighter variant, but with an additional 2000 litres of fuel, with the extra load provided for by the incorporation of two 1000 kg-thrust Jumo 004C engines with rocket-assisted take-off (RATO) units. No defensive armament was to be fitted, but bomb loads of either a 1000 kg bomb, two 500 kg bombs or a pair of 250 kg bombs could be carried. Maximum speed at 6000 m was 785 km/h, with a range of 1180 km.

Eight months after his 'bomb decree', at a conference on 27 October 1943, Hitler had remarked to *Großadmiral* Karl Dönitz, Commander-in-Chief of the Kriegsmarine, that a jet fighter able to carry bombs was a 'decisive factor'. The *Führer* envisaged jets streaking along an enemy beachhead, dropping their bombs into massed and apparently vulnerable ground troops. Göring is recorded as revealing what was perhaps his personal view on the subject at a meeting with Milch the next day, to whom he remarked, 'A fighter-bomber is a fighter that makes a virtue out of necessity'.

It seems his view had become a little more pragmatic by 2 November when attending a meeting with Messerschmitt at Regensburg. The Reichsmarschall wanted to know

On a cold day in the winter of 1944–45, and with the aid of a hydraulic trolley, Luftwaffe armourers load a 500 kg SC 500 bomb on to the 'Wikingerschiff' bomb rack of an Me 262A-2a. This aircraft carried out bomb-dropping trials before being assigned to I./KG 51 for operations in January 1945 (*EN Archive*)

how far an Me 262 could carry 'one or two bombs', and he relayed Hitler's vision of jet 'fighter-bombers' wreaking havoc among an enemy invasion force. Messerschmitt – perhaps artfully – responded that it was intended 'from the outset' that the Me 262 would be able to carry bombs of 250 kg to 1000 kg, although he did also state that the bomb racks and electrical installations had not, by that time, been prepared. When Göring pressed the aircraft designer as to just how long such a modification would take, Messerschmitt responded, 'Oh, not very long – two weeks, perhaps. It really isn't much of a problem, just a matter of fairing the [bomb] racks'. This was enough for the Reichsmarschall, who replied, 'That answers the *Führer*'s question'.

The very next day, Milch informed officials in the RLM that Messerschmitt had been told to build every Me 262, including those already in production, with mounts and electrics for bomb racks. With the exception of early prototypes, *all* such aircraft were to be able to be deployed as fighter-bombers. Today, this order should be viewed in context. Hitler may not have possessed a solid understanding of air strategy or operations, and his preference was always for offence not defence, but every other Luftwaffe combat aircraft had already proved itself adequately capable of carrying bombs or performing in the fighter-bomber role. Why, then, should the Me 262 be any different?

Hitler kept the pressure up on Göring. On 5 December his Luftwaffe adjutant, Oberstleutnant Nicolaus von Below, cabled the Reichsmarschall;

'The *Führer* has called our attention again to the tremendous importance of the production of jet-propelled aircraft for employment as fighter-bombers. It is imperative that the Luftwaffe have a number of jet fighter-bombers ready for front commitment by the spring of 1944. Any difficulties occasioned by labour and raw material shortages will be resolved by the exploitation of Luftwaffe resources, until existing shortages can be made up. The *Führer* feels that a delay in our jet aircraft programme would be tantamount to irresponsible negligence. The *Führer* has directed that bi-monthly written reports, the first of which was due on 15 November 1943, be made to him concerning the progress of the Me 262.'

23 May 1944 saw the commencement of a three-day conference on aircraft production chaired by Göring and held on the Obersalzberg to which several leading figures within the Luftwaffe had been summoned to attend. On the 24th, the question of the Me 262 found its way, inevitably, onto the agenda, this time over concerns relating to its build quality. Milch asked Oberstleutnant Siegfried Knemeyer, the Head of Air Technical Equipment in the RLM's Development Department, for his input. Knemeyer explained that the undercarriage on the Me 262 was not of sufficient strength, and that in order to deploy it as a fighter-bomber, weight would have to be lost. But that would mean needing to remove its nose armament, which would affect the centre of gravity.

Göring became aghast as he realised the significance of this, which, in effect, meant that despite Messerschmitt's assurances, the Me 262 had *not* been built as a fighter-bomber. Knemeyer poured further petrol onto the fire when he commented that, despite the order from Hitler, it had then been decreed that it was not necessary to fit the Me 262 with a bomb-rack 'immediately'. Evidently confusion reigned, and by the third day of the conference, by which time Professor Messerschmitt was in attendance, there was still some uncertainty between the two men as to the fixings for bomb racks.

Notwithstanding this, after the conference, Göring informed his staff that series production of the Me 262 was to be turned over to the production of a dedicated *bomber* variant – not a *fighter-bomber*. On 27 May, the Me 262 V10 became the first aircraft of the type to carry a bomb when it undertook an extended flight loaded with a 250 kg bomb.

On 22 June, just over a fortnight after the Allied landings in Normandy, Karl-Otto Saur, an engineer and head of the *Jägerstab* (the emergency committee formed to regenerate fighter production), informed a gathering of his officials;

A good view of one of the ETC 503 bomb racks fitted beneath an Me 262A-2a of 1./KG 51. Note that the upper gun ports have been faired over. The nose is in the white of the *Staffel* colour. Stencilling on the nose just beneath the camouflage demarcation line reads *Hier aufbocken* ('Jack up here') (*EN Archive*)

'Two days ago on the express order of the *Führer* another detailed discussion with him was held on the subject of the Me 262. Reichsmarschall Göring, Generalfeldmarschall Milch, General [Karl-Heinrich] Bodenschatz and Minister [Albert] Speer took part and I was also present. At this conference the *Führer* clearly outlined the situation. In its present form the Me 262 must be used in the first place as a very high-speed bomber only. It must be produced earlier and in larger numbers than present planning has allowed for.'

While future production was dealt with at high level, at Lechfeld, training had commenced in early June for a small cadre of pilots from 3./KG 51 under the command of Oberleutnant Eberhard Winkel, although simultaneously, an *Einsatzkommando* was also set up from elements of 3. *Staffel* headed by Major Wolfgang Schenck in order to develop operational tactics in advance of larger scale deployment.

Schenck was a very experienced unit commander and tactician, leading I./ZG 1 in the Soviet Union in strikes against enemy airfields and tanks. He was awarded the Oak Leaves to the Knight's Cross in October 1942 before being withdrawn from operations to take up a position within the RLM. At the end of January 1943, Schenck returned to operations as *Kommodore* of *Schlachtgeschwader* (SG) 2 in the Mediterranean. However he was wounded in action, and it was not until December 1943 that he returned to duties as *Inspizient der Schlachtflieger* before being reassigned once more, this time to the RLM's Technical Office.

By the end of June KG 51 had a total of seven aircraft on strength, including at least one of the new dedicated bomber variants, the A-2a. As the bomber version of the Me 262, the A-2 was to be equipped with two ETC 503A-1 bomb racks beneath the forward fuselage and a Revi 16D reflector gunsight designed for use with the reduced armament of two nose-mounted 30 mm MK 108 cannon. For bombing missions, the jet was to carry one 500 kg or two 250 kg bombs, or the equivalent weight in containers loaded with ten kilogramme anti-personnel bombs. Unlike in the Ju 88, KG 51's most commonly used aircraft throughout the war, there was no downward-looking bombsight, but after some degree of training it was felt that pilots should become accustomed to using the Revi for bombing.

By the end of June, the Allies had landed more than 750,000 troops in Normandy and some 40,000 German soldiers had been captured. Hitler was growing ever more impatient over delays to the debut of the Me 262 over the beaches. On 2 July 1944, Generalleutnant Karl Koller, Chief of the Luftwaffe Operations Staff, noted in his diary that, 'The *Führer* expects the *Einsatzkommando Me 262* (15 aircraft) to be ready for action soon'. Koller was tasked with determining the exact date. Yet in the very early hours of the 8th, Koller had a conversation with Generalleutnant Hermann Plocher, Chief of Staff of *Luftflotte* 3 based in France. Plocher told Koller that in his opinion, 'The range and penetration depth of the Me 262 as a bomber is too low for the West, as the forward airfields cannot be occupied'.

According to data furnished to *Luftflotte* 3 by technicians in Berlin in early June, the Me 262A-2a required a landing area of 1500 x 400 m, with reinforced strips on either side; permanent taxi tracks of 12 m; minimum obstacle clearance of 1:70 (and, if possible, 1:100) and a 'supplementary fuel installation' of 300 cubic metres, of which 100 cubic metres was to be near to the take-off point. None of this could be assured in France.

Finally, on 20 July – the day Hitler's *Wolfsschanze* (Wolf's Lair) headquarters at Rastenburg was rocked by Oberst Claus von Stauffenberg's bomb – the *Einsatzkommando*/KG 51 began its transfer from Lechfeld to Châteaudun, in France, with nine aircraft, its mission being to bomb the enemy beachhead in Normandy and to attack and harass Allied forces as they attempted to break out and advance on Caen.

By this time each pilot had made about four familiarisation and training flights in the Me 262, although results were to prove little better than those achieved by the interceptors of *Kdo. Nowotny*. Indeed, following a visit to France, and echoing the views of Plocher, Fritz Wendel was of the opinion that the range of the Me 262 bombers was insufficient for their missions since their base was located more than 100 km from the front on account of strong enemy fighter activity. But the whole point of the so-called '*Blitzbomber*' was its speed, and so it should have been the one aircraft that could evade Allied fighters.

From a technical perspective, the problem identified by Knemeyer in the meeting with Göring on 24 May manifested itself. Pilots found that when they dropped their bombs in shallow dives, stability problems ensued as a result of the centre of gravity shifting to the rear – a situation brought on by the introduction of additional fuel tanks. The only solution was to reduce tankage, which in turn adversely affected range. Furthermore, the Me 262s delivered to KG 51 lacked fuel gauges and suffered from faulty fuel pumps, but most astonishingly they had no bombsight suitable for use in a single-seat aircraft. Pilots had to resort to using the Revi reflector gunsight intended for fighters.

Evidently, doubt about the Me 262 lingered at the very highest levels of the German government, including with Albert Speer, the *Reichsminister* for Armaments and War Production. Generalleutnant Werner Kreipe, the newly appointed acting Chief of Staff of the Luftwaffe, was at Rastenburg on 18 August. He noted in his diary;

'At the *Wolfsschanze* for a meeting with Speer, Saur and Eschenauer on fighter production. Speer presses me about the Me 262. I am to talk the *Führer* out of the '*Blitzbomber*'. Speer wants to drill Hitler and negotiate hard with him. He sees clearly and soberly.'

Four days later, regardless of any concerns Plocher may have expressed about the Me 262's combat potential over France or the lack of available airfields within *Luftflotte* 3's jurisdiction,

Deadly cargo – SD 10A fragmentation bombs are loaded into the two wooden halves of an AB 250 bomb container. Such ordnance was used by the Me 262s of I. and II./KG 51 to drop on to 'soft-skinned' Allied transport columns and troop concentrations from low altitude (*EN Archive*)

the OKL advised the *Flotte* of the imminent arrival of a second *Schwarm* (a tactical formation of usually four aircraft) for the *Einsatzkommando*. Furthermore, the *Flotte* was to 'immediately determine further deployment and alternative airfields so that necessary measures for stockpiling can be initiated. Make the airfields operational as quickly as possible, as the failure of the current single airfield will jeopardise operations'.

On 24 August, the *Einsatzkommando* (*Kdo.*) *Schenck* reported that it had four operational pilots and four Me 262A-2as, of which three were serviceable.

In what may have been the *Kommando*'s combat debut, on the morning of the 25th, these four aircraft took off from Juvincourt to attack targets in the area of the bend in the Seine, northwest of Paris. All aircraft returned after midday. A second operation was flown in the mid-afternoon by the four jets against the same target, but one of them made an emergency landing close to the front and was lost.

Between 0934–0942 hrs on the 26th, the remaining three jets took off to attack troop concentrations on the left bank of the Seine in the first of several sorties that day. Targets included enemy assemblies in woods near Chailly-en-Bierre and on the road between Melun and Fontainebleau. The town of Melun was targeted with two SC 500s, while the area around it was hit with two AB 500 *Abwurfbehälter* (containers) loaded with SD 10 *Splitterbombe* and *Dickwandig* thick-walled fragmentation bombs. At Mantes and in the area northeast of Bonnières-sur-Seine, the jets made a horizontal approach at 3000–4000 m, each dropping an AB 500 into a wooded area southeast of Bonnières.

The subsequently expanded *Kommando*'s initial missions, flown mainly with Me 262A-1a fighters rigged with bomb racks, met with little success. Fritz Wendel did not attribute this failure to pilots or tactics, but rather 'In level flight, the Revi was useless for accurate bombing. Pinpoint targets could not be hit. *Kdo. Schenck* was, therefore, unable to claim any tactical successes'.

Hardly had the *Kommando* commenced operations than on the evening of the 28th the proximity of Allied forces to the airfield at Juvincourt forced a move to Ath-Chièvres, southwest of Brussels in Belgium. During the transfer flight Oberfeldwebel Hieronymous Lauer of 3./KG 51 was forced to fly his Me 262 with its undercarriage lowered due to a blend of malfunction and pilot error. Unfortunately, Lauer was spotted and attacked by a pair of patrolling P-47s from the USAAF's 78th FG.

The American pilots went into a 45-degree dive, reaching 475 mph before they began to overtake the jet. Lauer began a series of evasive turns just as Maj Joseph Myers in the lead P-47 opened fire. The Me 262 crashed into a field near Haaltert, southwest of Aalst, before rounds from the P-47's guns actually hit his aircraft. Lauer escaped injury, but his was the first Me 262 to be claimed by Allied fighters. According to Wendel, 'The two starter fuel tanks caught fire and the pilot made a forced landing on the main undercarriage with the nosewheel retracted. The badly damaged aircraft was later blown up'.

With the arrival of September, Field Marshal Bernard Montgomery's 21st Army Group broke out of northwest France and advanced steadily across Belgium to close on the port of Antwerp. After two days at Ath-Chièvres, the three pilots and operational aircraft of *Kdo. Schenck* had arrived at Volkel, in the Neteherlands. This small contingent comprised Schenck, Leutnant Klaus Jäger and Oberfeldwebel Gerd Gittmann, the latter two pilots from 3./KG 51. The shot-down Oberfeldwebel Lauer and the wounded Feldwebel Horst Schulz, also of 3./KG 51, made their way to Volkel by alternative means.

At Volkel, the pilots found an 1800 m runway sufficient for their needs, but much of the airfield's infrastructure had been destroyed by Allied bombing. Within three days of the *Kommando*'s arrival, this situation was compounded when 130 Lancasters bombed the field again. Two jets were destroyed, including Schenck's aircraft. Shortly after, the *Kommando* moved once more, this time to Rheine.

Having taken off from the new base on 8 September, Leutnant Rolf Weidemann of 3./KG 51, flying an Me 262A-2a, was shot down and killed by British AA fire northeast of Diest, in Belgium, while strafing troops with his MK 108 cannon from a height of 150 m. Weidemann had collected his aircraft from Lechfeld just two days previously.

The next day, the *Einsatzkommando* KG 51 reported five Me 262s on strength. Following a weather reconnaissance flight by one jet to the Maastricht area, four Messerschmitts again attacked Diest, dropping four AB 500s loaded with SD 10s, but the pilots were unable to observe effects. Further attacks were not possible due to the deteriorating weather. The following morning, apparently reinforced by pilots and aircraft, a formation of 15 Me 262s from *Kdo. Schenck* attacked the road from Huy towards the west of Liège, the pilots observing hits on buildings southwest of the city and on the road from Liège to the west. On the 10th, Oberleutnant Werner Gärtner of 3. *Staffel* was reported missing when his Me 262 was hit by AA fire near Gomze, 11 km southwest of Verviers.

On 11 September ten Me 262s of the *Kommando* transferred temporarily to Schleswig, Wittmundhafen and Achmer, from where they mounted four attacks against Liège and enemy canal crossings near Beeringen. Explosions were observed around the canal. In the early afternoon of the 12th, the Me 262A-2a of Unteroffizier Herbert Schnauder from 3./KG 51 was hit by AA fire as he flew over the viaduct near Elden, 3.5 km southwest of Arnhem. Undertaking a ferry flight from Volkel to Rheine at the time, Schnauder was killed.

Five of the seven Me 262s available to *Kdo. Schenck* on 13 September made attacks during the early morning in the Lommel area. Evidently Oberfeldwebel Lauer had recovered from his traumatic experience over Belgium a few days earlier, for he was one of two pilots who attacked troop concentrations north of Hechtel on the Maas and on the Scheldt Canal. Effects were not observed. Orders also reached the unit that, on instructions of the *Führer* himself, enemy troop assemblies were to be attacked in the Beverlo area.

Fritz Wendel made a return visit to the unit on or around 13 September. He reported;

'During my visit, attacks were flown repeatedly against Liège. The target was normally approached at 4000 m, the bombs being dropped in a steep dive. The distance from the air base to the target was 230 km. On return, also made at 4000 m, the aircraft's main fuel tanks still contained an average of 350 litres each. The normal flight time was exactly 50 minutes. According to the pilots, all bombs hit targets somewhere within the town. In one case a road was hit. I am not in a position to judge the military value of these operations.

'Two further losses occurred during my visit, the pilots failing to return from an attack on Liège. No news about the fate of the aircraft had been received before I departed. It can be assumed that the two pilots flew off in the wrong direction and came down behind enemy lines. These losses were all due to faulty navigation, an opinion unanimously shared by the pilots.'

Later in the month, attacks were made in the Nijmegen and Arnhem areas where Allied airborne landings were taking place. As with earlier operations, most of the attacks in the Allied drop and landing zones were made with aircraft fitted with single AB 500 containers holding SD 10 anti-personnel bombs, although on occasion aircraft would carry two SD 250 semi armour-piercing bombs. At this time the *Kommando* reported an operational strength of 11 aircraft and 12 crews.

Throughout the gloomy autumn of 1944, what was formally known as *Einsatzkommando* I./KG 51 (effectively 3. *Staffel*) would struggle to provide badly needed air support to the German armies battling in the West. However, with their bases under continual attack from Allied fighters, against whom only the Me 262's speed was the saving grace, and with a shortage of fuel and bombs, this would prove challenging. The *Geschwader* had calculated that 65 tons of J2 fuel were needed to train just one pilot.

On 26 September, the unit apparently having received reinforcements, 20 Me 262s attacked targets in the Nijmegen area during the afternoon and evening. Troop columns were bombed using nine AB 500/SD 10 bomb combinations and 11 AB 500/SD 4s, but effects were not observed.

To the end of the month, the *Einsatzkommando* I./KG 51 maintained a relatively high sortie rate. On the 27th the unit was issued orders by *Gefechtsverband Hallensleben* to strike at enemy assembly points in the area south of Nijmegen. Three Me 262s took off, but two jets were forced to break off early, and while the third dropped its bomb, the effects of the weapon could not be determined because of the adverse weather. One machine was damaged on landing due to a collapsed nosewheel. On 28 September Me 262s of I./KG 51 flew 34 sorties against Nijmegen, although one aircraft had to break off early because of undercarriage problems that forced its pilot to jettison his bombs. Although an area south of the town was struck with 33 AB 500/SD 10 ordnance combinations, the presence of fighters from the 2nd Tactical Air Force (TAF) prevented further operations.

Throughout September, KG 51 was assigned 46 Me 262As and two-seat Me 262B-1s, but a lack of aircraft delayed II. *Gruppe* from starting conversion by one month – the whole of September. Furthermore, the need to maintain aircraft operating over the Nijmegen/Arnhem area would prevent I. *Gruppe* from becoming fully operational in a single location until the end of October.

The *Kommodore* of KG 51, Oberstleutnant Wolf Dietrich Meister, arrived at Lechfeld on the 29th with Major im Generalstab Richard Schubert, a technical officer on Göring's staff who was on a fact-finding mission to ascertain why so few Me 262s were operational. Meister and Schubert took off in one of the unit's two-seat Me 262B-1as on a flight over the airfield. During take-off, one of the RATO units fell away from the jet and hit the fuselage near the forward cockpit, which was occupied by Schubert. The hydraulics were damaged and the aircraft made a crash-landing.

From the end of September, I./KG 51 mounted reasonably consistent operations against the 2nd TAF airfields at Chiévres, Eindhoven, Nijmegen, Volkel and Grave using predominantly SD 250 *Sprengbomben* and AB 250 fragmentation containers.

By early October the *Einsatzkommando* must have received further aircraft, for on the 2nd, from around 0630 hrs, no fewer than 35 Me 262s attacked various enemy troop assembly points around Nijmegen. Two of the jets were forced to break off, but the rest made it to the target area and released 11 AB 500/SD 10 combinations and 22 AB 500/SD 1s.

During the first days of October, *Kdo. Schenck* continued to strike at Allied airfields and troop concentrations, as German ground forces launched attacks north of the Waal against the British Army's XXX Corps, while southeast of Nijmegen further attacks were made against the US Army's 82nd Airborne Division. However with relatively few aircraft operationally ready at any one time and no effective bombsights, its contribution to the German war effort was little more than derisory. An Allied report commented of the *Kommando*'s efforts as follows;

'They come in at dawn or just after, or at dusk and during the first few hours of darkness. Total number of bombs dropped has been small. There seems to be little coordination of effort, and aircraft come in singly or in groups of two or three. AA fire undoubtedly prevents accurate bombing. They drop bombs from considerable heights (about 10,000 ft), many of which are anti-personnel. During darkness, HE [high explosive] bombing by Me 262s is more normal.'

Towards the end of October 1944, *Kdo. Schenck* was officially re-incorporated into I./KG 51. By the end of the month it had received approximately 25 Me 262s and had flown a total of 163 missions involving 400 individual flights. Some pilots had flown up to six missions in a single day. Mission frequency would have been higher had it not been for the recurrence of extremely bad weather over the target areas. The unit reported three jets as total losses due to combat with the enemy and four lost due to non-combat reasons. Command of the *Geschwader* passed from Major Wolf-Dietrich Meister to Oberstleutnant Wolfgang Schenck on 21 October.

In one mission, mounted on 7 November, 16 Me 262s were ordered to operate against targets from Rheine. Hauptmann Rudolf Abrahamczik, Leutnant Oswald von Ritter-Rittershain, Oberfeldwebel Karl-Heinz Petersen and Leutnant Heinrich Haeffner, all of 2./KG 51 at Hopsten, were instructed to fly a mission with 3. *Staffel* from Rheine. Haeffner, the *Schwarmführer*, had to fly in a substitute machine since his usual aircraft was not functioning properly.

At 1305 hrs the four pilots took off from Hopsten and flew through bad weather and poor visibility to Rheine, where they landed some 15 minutes later. However, because of the worsening conditions, the mission was scrubbed and the pilots were forced to abandon their jets at Rheine and return to Hopsten by road. Upon returning to collect their aircraft, it was discovered that Haeffner's Me 262 had been sabotaged, and the evidence pointed to dissident Italian workers.

From early November to mid-December the Me 262s of I. and II./KG 51 (the latter *Gruppe* having completed transition to the Me 262 in mid-November) carried out regular small-scale attacks on Allied transport columns and positions in the eastern Netherlands and along the Dutch–German border area. An unnamed pilot of KG 51 captured by the Allies described what it was like to fly Me 262 bombing missions at this time;

'Briefing usually was very short, lasting from five to ten minutes. Information given was concerned only with the target and its location. There was no orientation on Flak or other factors affecting the mission. We were left to figure out our routes to and from the target and the altitudes to be flown.

'The deepest penetration Me 262s made with bombs was 250 km flying at an altitude of 4000 m. The formation flown to the target was usually of four aircraft abreast, with 25–30 m between wingtips. Speed to the target was about 675 km/h. The usual altitude was 4000 m, and each aircraft carried two 250 kg bombs under the nose. Prior to January 1945, Hitler's personal order forbade any Me 262 flying below 4000 m. The serious effect of this flying altitude on bombing accuracy caused continuous complaints from the pilots, but it was not until the end of January that the order was changed to allow pilots to go down to an altitude they considered safe.

'When Allied fighters were encountered en route to the target, the Me 262s usually increased speed and easily climbed away. Flak was evaded quite easily by weaving from side-to-side. The maximum diving angle of the Me 262 with bombs was 35 degrees. We dived from 4000 m to 1000 m, but never much lower. Care was taken to prevent the airspeed exceeding 920 km/h, since the Me 262 was red-lined at 950 km/h. Care was also exercised to empty the rear 600-litre tank before the dive. This was necessary because the release of bombs with a full rear tank caused the nose of the aircraft to pitch up very suddenly, either knocking out the pilot or throwing the machine into an uncontrollable spin.

'Our pilots used the old Revi gunsight which was supposedly accurate to within 35 to 40 m. Following release of our bombs, the Me 262s returned home at between 1000 and 1200 m, with a distance of 60 to 90 m between aircraft.' (*text continues on page 45*)

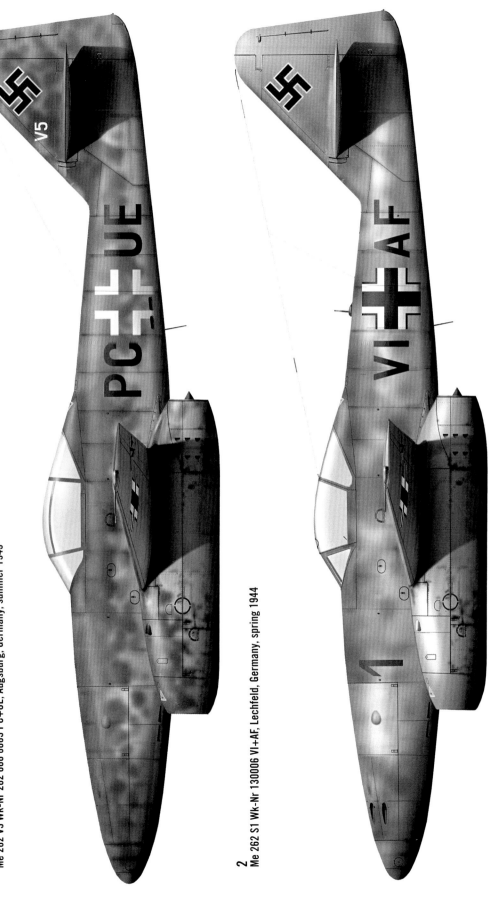

COLOUR PLATES

1
Me 262 V5 Wk-Nr 262 000 0005 PC+UE, Augsburg, Germany, summer 1943

2
Me 262 S1 Wk-Nr 130006 VI+AF, Lechfeld, Germany, spring 1944

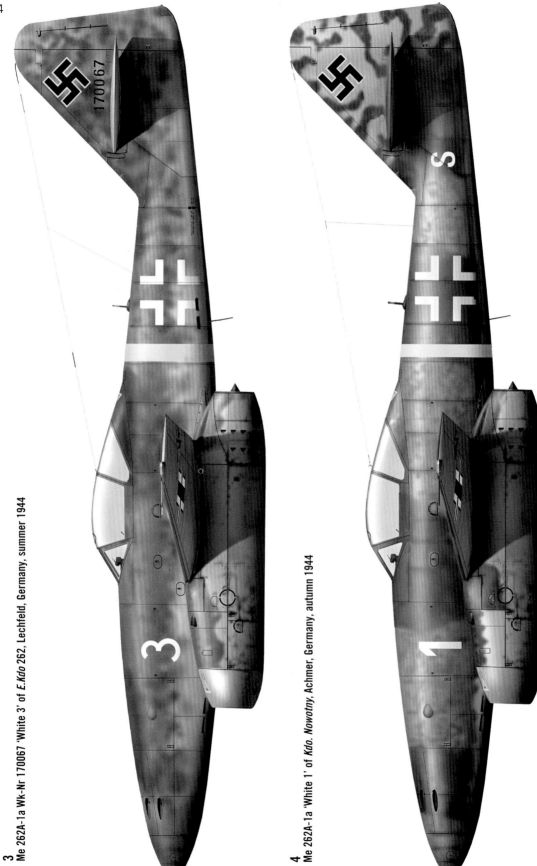

3
Me 262A-1a Wk-Nr 170067 'White 3' of *E.Kdo* 262, Lechfeld, Germany, summer 1944

4
Me 262A-1a 'White 1' of *Kdo. Nowotny*, Achmer, Germany, autumn 1944

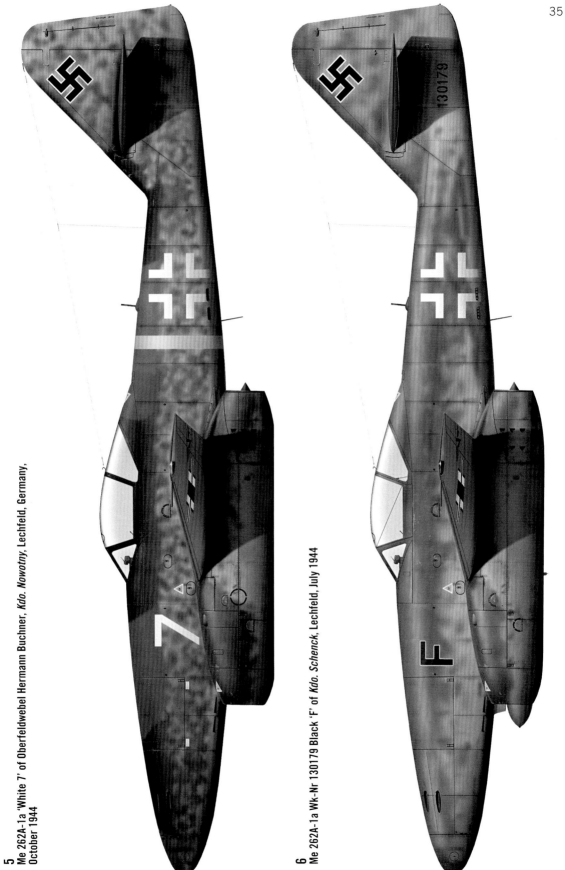

5
Me 262A-1a 'White 7' of Oberfeldwebel Hermann Buchner, *Kdo. Nowotny*, Lechfeld, Germany,
October 1944

6
Me 262A-1a Wk-Nr 130179 Black 'F' of *Kdo. Schenck*, Lechfeld, July 1944

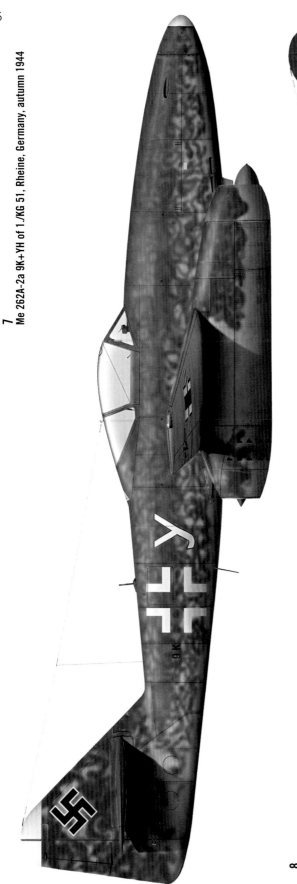

7
Me 262A-2a 9K+YH of 1./KG 51, Rheine, Germany, autumn 1944

8 Me 262A-1a 'Green 1' of Major Rudolf Sinner, *Stab* III./JG 7, Brandenburg-Briest, Germany, January 1945

9
Me 262 A-1a Wk-Nr 111588 'White 5' of 11./JG 7, Brandenburg-Briest, Germany, January 1945

10
Me 262A-2a Wk-Nr 170064 9K+BK of 2./KG 51, Rheine, Germany, October 1944

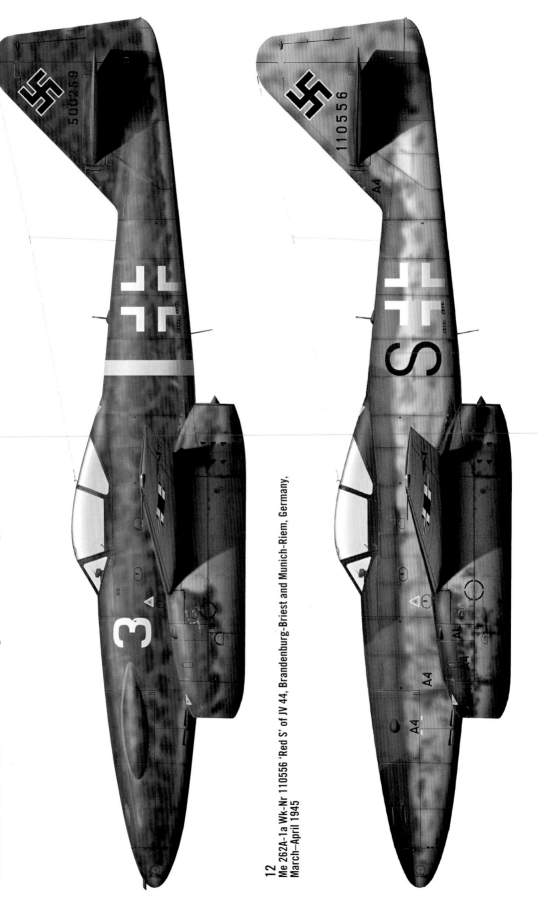

11
Me 262A-1a/U3 Wk-Nr 500259 'White 3' of 1./NAG 6, Eger or Lechfeld, Germany, March 1945

12
Me 262A-1a Wk-Nr 110556 'Red S' of JV 44, Brandenburg-Briest and Munich-Riem, Germany,
March–April 1945

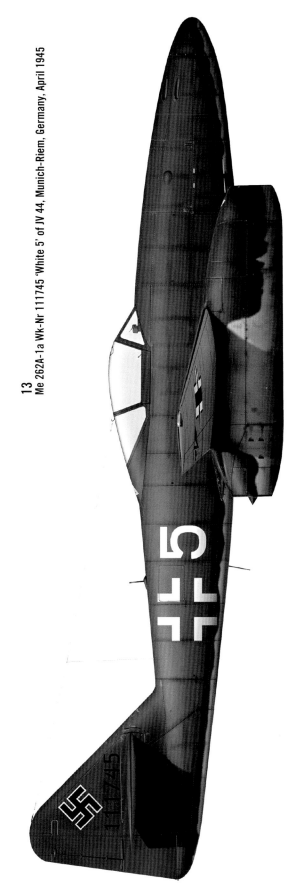

13
Me 262A-1a Wk-Nr 111745 'White 5' of IV 44, Munich-Riem, Germany, April 1945

14
Me 262A-2a Wk-Nr 111685 'White F' of 1./KG 51, Hopsten, Germany, March 1945

15
Me 262A-1 Wk-Nr 111620 'B3+GR' of 7./KG(J) 54, Neuburg/Donau, Germany, February 1945

16
Me 262B-1a Wk-Nr 111643 'B3+ZM' of 4./KG(J) 54, Czechoslovakia, May 1945

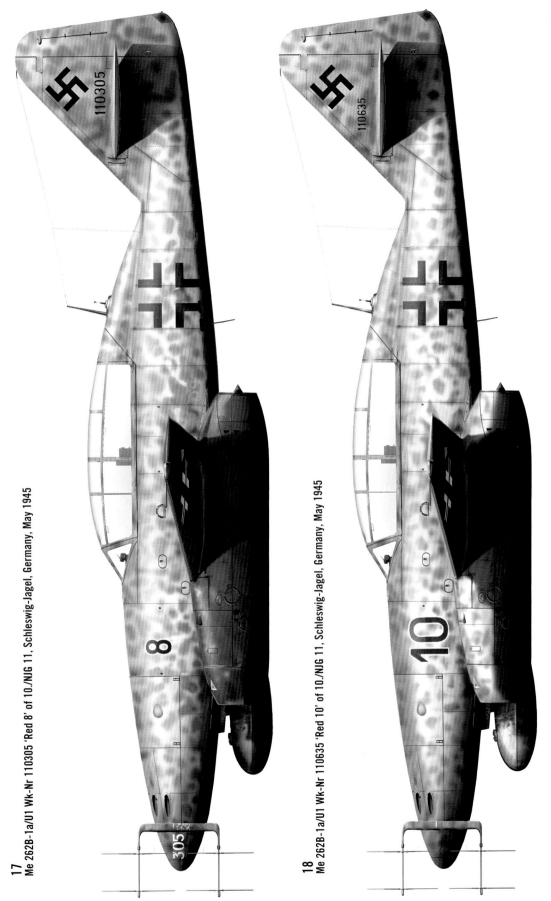

17
Me 262B-1a/U1 Wk-Nr 110305 'Red 8' of 10./NJG 11, Schleswig-Jagel, Germany, May 1945

18
Me 262B-1a/U1 Wk-Nr 110635 'Red 10' of 10./NJG 11, Schleswig-Jagel, Germany, May 1945

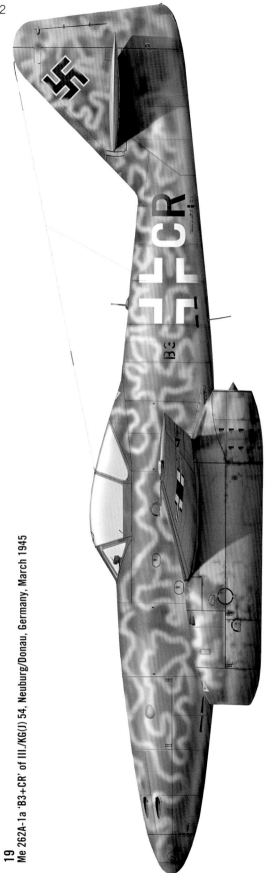

19
Me 262A-1a 'B3+CR' of III./KG(J) 54, Neuburg/Donau, Germany, March 1945

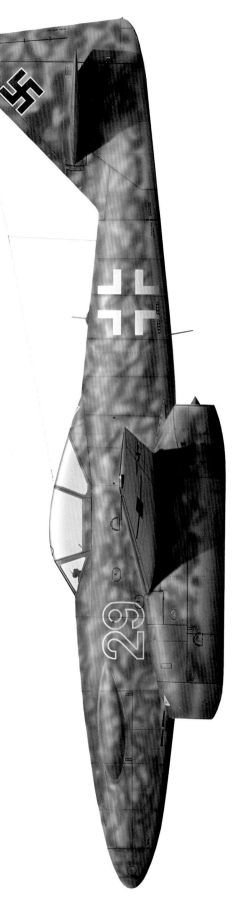

20
Me 262A-1a/U3 Wk-Nr 500853 '29' probably of 1./NAG 6, Lechfeld, Germany, May 1945

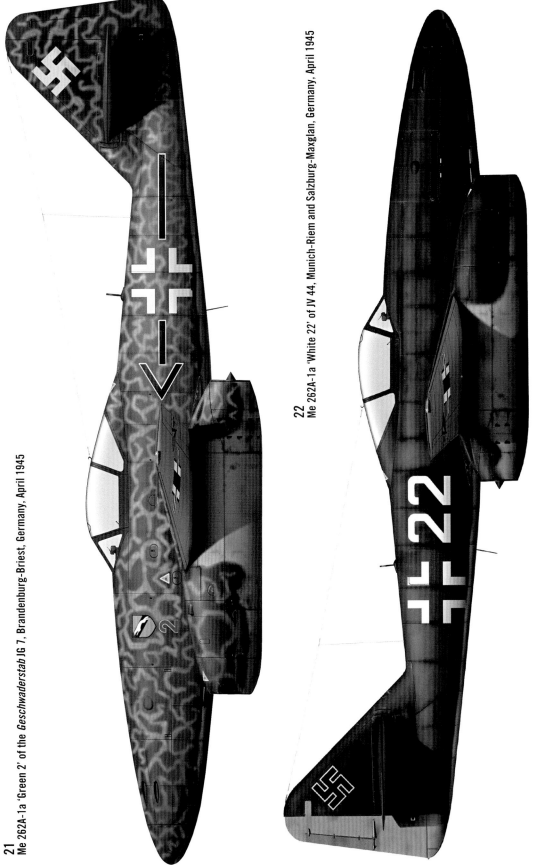

21
Me 262A-1a 'Green 2' of the *Geschwaderstab* JG 7, Brandenburg-Briest, Germany, April 1945

22
Me 262A-1a 'White 22' of JV 44, Munich-Riem and Salzburg-Maxglan, Germany, April 1945

44

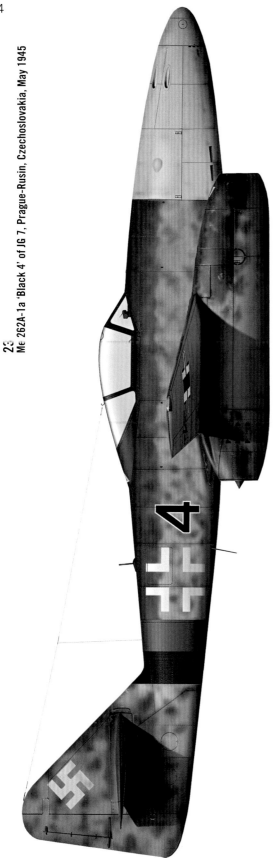

23
Me 262A-1a 'Black 4' of JG 7, Prague-Rusin, Czechoslovakia, May 1945

24
Me 262A-2a Wk-Nr 111712 of JV 44, Munich-Riem and Innsbruck-Hötting, Germany,
April–May 1945

Visible here is the hawser connecting the port mainwheel of Me 262A-1a/U3 'White 3' of III./EJG 2 with a *Kettenkrad* tow tractor at Lechfeld in early 1945. A mechanic sits in the cockpit as the aircraft is towed over the concrete taxiway, a process which saved fuel. The bulged fairing on the nose to allow fitment of one of the aircraft's two Rb 50/30 cameras is also visible (*EN Archive*)

With considerable experience from the Eastern Front, the Austrian Knight's Cross-holder Oberleutnant Herward Braunegg was appointed to lead the first *Sonderkommando* tasked with flying and evaluating the Me 262 as a reconnaissance and photo-reconnaissance aircraft under operational conditions. The small unit would carry his name as *Kdo. Braunegg*, later known as *Kdo. Panther* (*Author Collection*)

Under the codename '*Wacht am Rhein*' ('Watch on the Rhine'), the last great German offensive in the West began in the early morning of 16 December 1944. It was a plan devised by Hitler, who wanted to drive an armoured wedge between the Allies by thrusting through the forests and hill country of the Ardennes to retake Antwerp. To succeed, however, it was vital for the Germans to have as much air support as possible. The next day I./KG 51 went into action in poor weather, with six Me 262s strafing American ground forces in the Saint Vith area.

Meanwhile, on 17 December, a new Me 262 unit commenced operations from Schwäbisch Hall. *Kdo. Panther* would play an important part in the preparations for the German offensive by deploying its camera-equipped jets over the Allied rear. The unit's aircraft would be able to roam virtually at will over Allied lines, gathering vital photographic coverage of enemy troop dispositions and the crossings over the Meuse.

Kdo. Panther has been issued with the Me 262A-1a/U3, which was a modification of the standard fighter with two Rb 50/30 cameras installed in the nose, angled outwards at 11 degrees and controlled by an intervalometer with an attached drive motor. Because the cameras were too large to fit cleanly within the nose compartment, small horizontal teardrop fairings were fitted to both left and right gun access panels to cover the protruding areas, and the usual gun ports found on the A-1a were faired over. Two small square glazed panels were provided for the camera lenses beneath the fuselage on either side of the nosewheel well. The variant also incorporated a single MK 108 cannon mounted in the extreme nose, with its muzzle protruding level with the tip. Because of its superior speed in comparison to Allied fighters, the Me 262 was an ideal aircraft to provide short-range reconnaissance.

Since June 1944, *Kdo. Panther* had been under the command of Oberleutnant Herward Braunegg, an Austrian reconnaissance pilot and Knight's Cross-holder who had served in the Soviet Union as a *Staffelkapitän* with *Nahaufklärungsgruppe* (NAGr.) 9. Initially known as *Kdo. Braunegg*, the unit was redesignated *Kdo. Panther* on 15 December, at which point it reported a strength of 11 pilots and six Me 262A-1a/U3s. Despite this, it would be rare for more than four aircraft to be operational at one time.

Two days later, for its debut mission, the *Kommando* reconnoitered the Trier–Saarbrücken–Lauterburg area, and on the 22nd it mounted four sorties in the Mühlhausen–Basel–Delle–Weissenburg–Lautenburg–Bitsch areas. Three more sorties were flown on 24 December in the Saarlautern area.

Towards the end of 1944, Generalmajor Karl-Henning von Barsewisch, the *General der Aufklärer*, had proposed to equip another reconnaissance unit, NAGr. 1, with the Me 262 after the RLM had cancelled the proposed high-performance/high-altitude Bf 109H-2/R2 reconnaissance-fighter in favour of the Me 262A-1a/U3. This was in addition to an order issued back on 5 August to create a 'new' NAGr. 6 from elements of reconnaissance units which previously had seen operations on the southern sector of the Eastern Front and around Stalingrad. 1./NAGr. 6 was duly formed at Bayreuth-Bindlach from 3.(H)/Aufkl.Gr.21 and 2./NAGr. 6 at the same location from 12./Aufkl.Gr.12. Thus, by December, *Stab*/NAGr. 6 was equipped with Me 262s but was non-operational under *Luftflotte*

Reich, and 1. and 2./NAGr. 6 were forming up and were non-operational under *Luftflotte* 10.

It was, admittedly, a low-key start to Luftwaffe reconnaissance operations with the Me 262, but the value of these small units would be very much realised in the coming months when the intelligence that they provided to the German military high command and its commanders in the field would be rated extremely highly.

On Christmas Day, the main target for the jet bombers of KG 51 was Liège. The Me 262A 1a of Oberleutnant Hans-Georg Lamle, *Staffelführer* of 4./KG 51, was firstly hit by British AA fire while in the target area near Liège. Then, on his return to base, Lamle was intercepted and shot down by a Spitfire flown by Flt Lt Jack Boyle of No 411 Sqn RCAF near Heesch. His jet hit the ground near Erp, 107 km north of Liège.

Liège was targeted by KG 51 again on the 27th, but there were also further missions to Nijmegen, where, despite heavy anti-aircraft fire, Feldwebel Johann Trenke of 6./KG 51 made a gliding attack and dropped two bombs into the town centre. His *Staffel* comrade, Fahnenjunker-Oberfeldwebel Wilhelm Haase, also attempted to reach Nijmegen but ran into enemy fighters. Having evaded them, he instead attacked troop targets on the Hasselt–Zonhoven road.

Hampered by Allied air power, weather and terrain, starved of fuel and meeting firm opposition, the German assault in the Ardennes, having penetrated 112 km at its deepest point, but still far short of Antwerp, faltered and stopped on 30 December 1944. The last German attempt to close the Bastogne corridor had failed, and with the initiative now lost, *General der Panzertruppe* Hasso von Manteuffel's 5. *Panzer Armee* abandoned any hope of further offensive action.

A senior NCO glances at one of the groundcrew prior to unloading the Rb 50/30 cameras from the open panels (through which the MK 108 cannon would otherwise be accessed) of Me 262A-1a/U3 'White 3' of III./EJG 2 at Lechfeld. The aircraft is armed with just one repositioned cannon, the barrel of which is seen protruding from the nose. The *Kettenkrad* will probably perform the dual function of towing the jet back to its dispersal and delivering cameras to the *Gruppe*'s photographic development section. This Me 262 carried out reconnaissance trials before being assigned to NAGr. 6 (*EN Archive*)

An NCO hands a precious Rb 50/30 camera, which he has just removed from the nose bay of Me 262A-1a/U3 'White 3' of III./EJG 2, to a mechanic, who will deliver it to the unit's photographic development section. Timely processing of film was of vital importance to German military commanders on the ground (*EN Archive*)

CHAPTER FOUR

A NEW FIGHTER WING

Me 262 interceptors of JG 7 at Brandenburg-Briest in early 1945. The nearest aircraft is finished in a standard late-war mottle, but appears to have no tactical number or *Geschwader* emblem, possibly indicating a newly delivered machine. The centre jet has a more unusual striped scheme, while the furthest Me 262 features a dark green finish with a lower demarcation line and lighter undersurfaces. Note the rare solid white Hakenkreuze on the tail surfaces (*EN Archive*)

In mid-November 1944, Generalleutnant Galland took steps to reorganise, consolidate and expand the jet interceptor force. In some ways recent events had served to support him in this. At the beginning of the month Hitler had finally given his permission for the Me 262 to be built as a fighter, but under the strict proviso that the aircraft should be able to carry at least one 250 kg bomb if necessary. This gave Galland the opportunity to move ahead with the establishment of a jet-equipped fighter unit which would be assigned the redundant designation JG 7 under which it had originally been intended to form a new piston-engined wing equipped with the latest types of Fw 190 or Bf 109. This intention had been frustrated, however, primarily by a shortage of aircraft arising as a result of the need to replace losses in existing units.

A few days later, on 12 November, matters were confirmed when OKL issued official orders that JG 7 was *not* to be equipped with piston-engined aircraft. Around the same time, Galland appointed Oberst Johannes Steinhoff as *Kommodore* of the new *Geschwader*.

Steinhoff had enjoyed a reputation as one of the Luftwaffe's most accomplished fighter aces and formation leaders. He was awarded the Knight's Cross on 30 August 1941 and was appointed *Kommandeur* of II./JG 52 on 28 February 1942. By 31 August of that year, Steinhoff had chalked up 100 aerial kills, and he received the Oak Leaves two days later. On 24 March 1943 he was transferred from the Eastern Front to Tunisia, where he assumed command of JG 77. Steinhoff led the unit from North Africa through the campaign over Sicily and Italy, engaging USAAF heavy bombers and their escorts, against which his personal score continued to accumulate. In late July 1944 he was awarded the Swords to his Knight's Cross in recognition of his 167th aerial victory.

But in the autumn of 1944, Steinhoff had become persona non grata with the Luftwaffe leadership on account of his support for Galland, whose own star was falling as a result of what Göring saw as his failings in the management of the daylight fighter force in the air battles to defend the Reich. Galland had other supporters, and a small clique of veteran fighter unit leaders formed – among them Steinhoff who were dismayed and angry at what *they* saw as Göring's unreasonable and unrealistic handling of matters.

It was against such a background that Steinhoff took command. On 19 November, what remained of *Kommando Nowotny* at Lechfeld was redesignated III./JG 7 and transferred to Brandenburg-Briest, to the west of Berlin, where it joined the *Geschwaderstab*. The *Gruppe* was augmented by flying, ground and technical personnel from the recently disbanded KG 1 'Hindenburg', whose honour title the new *Geschwader* would adopt for a brief period. Simultaneously, the originally planned I./JG 7, to be formed from II./KG 1, was slated to be redesignated as II./JG 7 on 24 November, with 1., 2., 3. and 4./JG 7 forming a new 5., 6., 7. and 8./JG 7.

As *Kommandeur* of the first Me 262 *Gruppe* to be formed (III./JG 7), Steinhoff was assigned Major Erich Hohagen, a recipient of the Knight's Cross in 1941 who had accumulated several thousand hours flying on some 60 different types. A veteran of combat over the Western and Eastern Fronts with JG 2 and JG 27, his total of 55 victories gained from more than 500 missions included 13 highly prized four-engined bombers. In the autumn of 1944, Hohagen had been forced to belly-land his stricken Bf 109, during which he had ploughed into a bank and smashed his head on the Messerschmitt's reflector sight. A surgeon had later replaced a piece of his skull with plastic and pulled the skin back together, resulting in a facial disfiguration.

Major Erich Hohagen peers down from the cockpit of Me 262 'White 2' during his brief period of training on the aircraft with III./ EJG 2 at Lechfeld in late 1944. Compared to the photograph on page 16, the aircraft now appears worn and weathered. Hohagen was a popular officer and recipient of the Knight's Cross who had been credited with 55 victories in more than 500 missions, including claims for 13 four-engined bombers. He would serve briefly with JG 7, before joining Galland's JV 44 (*EN Archive*)

The former officer cadre of *Kommando Nowotny* was used to command the component *Staffeln*, with Oberleutnant Joachim Weber, who had commanded 1./*Kdo. Nowotny* following the death of Oberleutnant Bley in a take-off accident, assuming command of 9./JG 7, while Leutnant Schall took over 10./JG 7 and Hauptmann Eder led 11. *Staffel*. The new *Geschwader* would fall under the tactical control of 1. *Jagddivision* and would operate in the defence of the airspace over Berlin and northeastern Germany.

In his memoirs, Steinhoff recalled how the unit received partly assembled Me 262s delivered by rail from southern Germany which were then fully assembled by teams of Luftwaffe and Messerschmitt mechanics. 'By the end of November', he wrote, 'we were in the air, training in flights of three and in small formations'.

Following the establishment of III./JG 7, another *Gruppe*, I./JG 7, was formed on 27 November at Königsberg from pilots and personnel of the Bf 109-equipped II./JG 3, with 5./JG 3 becoming 1./JG 7, 7./JG 3 becoming 2./JG 7 and 8./JG 3 becoming 3./JG 7. The illustrious JG 5 veteran Major Theodor Weissenberger, a holder of the Oak Leaves to the Knight's Cross, was appointed *Kommandeur*. He had been credited with his 200th victory on 25 July 1944 while JG 5 had been serving in Normandy.

Appointed as *Staffelkapitäne* of I./JG 7 were Oberleutnant Hans Grünberg, a Stalingrad veteran, former *Staffelkapitän* of 5./JG 3 and a Knight's Cross-holder with 77 victories to his credit for 1. *Staffel*, Oberleutnant Fritz Stehle from ZG 26 for 2. *Staffel* and Oberleutnant Hans Waldmann, who had served as *Kapitän* of 4./JG 52 and 8./JG 3, for 3. *Staffel*. Also a recipient of the Knight's Cross, Waldmann had accounted for the destruction of no fewer than 32 Il-2s over the Eastern Front.

Training proved dangerous, especially for pilots who grappled with flying a twin-engined aircraft powered by a new form of propulsion and which had to be handled carefully during take-off and landing. Steinhoff recounted;

'Naturally, the flying qualities of the Me 262 were influenced by the high wing loading (280 kg per square metre) and the low thrust (850 kg per engine, but only 3.6 kg of weight). We needed a 1200 m runway, and the acceleration after take-off was so slow that during the first few minutes the aircraft had to be nursed.

'At cruising speed – something over 800 km/h – the Me 262 handled well, except that the controls needed much force, particularly during violent manoeuvres – oil pressure controls, as used on modern jets, were then unknown. Similarly, though their absence nowadays is also unthinkable, we had to do without dive brakes, and this considerably limited our manoeuvrability particularly as regards loops and turns. In order to reduce speed, it was necessary to reduce power, which again, at high altitude, could lead into a compressor stall.

'The other weakness was the Jumo 004 turbines. Their blades could not withstand the temperatures sometimes reached, and this, together with faults in the induction system, often caused them to burn up. The life of these engines was therefore only 20 hours and the accident rate was high.'

On 26 November, III./JG 7 suffered the loss of one of the original *Kommando Nowotny* pilots, Leutnant Alfred Schreiber of 9. *Staffel*, who

Oberst Johannes Steinhoff, the first commander of JG 7, did not last long in his post. The highly decorated fighter commander was replaced because of his empathy with Generalleutnant Adolf Galland. He would go on to serve with the dismissed *General der Jagdflieger* in JV 44 (*Author Collection*)

was killed when his Me 262 crashed near Lechfeld. The following month, Feldwebel Erwin Eichhorn, one of the first Luftwaffe pilots to fly the Me 262 with *E.Kdo* 262, was also lost as a result of an accident at Lechfeld.

As if the losses incurred during training and/or as a result of accidents were not enough, the supply of aircraft was painfully slow. Of those that did arrive in November–December, several were lost as a result of Allied bombing raids either at Briest or on other airfields. During the month of December, III./JG 7 had taken delivery of 41 Me 262s, while I. *Gruppe* received just two A-1as converted as two-seat trainers – this from a total factory output that month of 114 aircraft, plus 17 repaired machines. Nor did the winter weather help. When four of III./JG 7's freshly trained pilots were sent on 16 December from Lechfeld northeast to Messerschmitt at Obertraubling to collect Me 262s for onward ferrying to Briest, they were frustrated in their efforts by bad weather. They did not reach JG 7's base until Christmas.

Meanwhile, the *Geschwader* had flown its first operations, albeit in very small numbers. On 2 December, Leutnant Weber of 9./JG 7 shot down an F-5 of the 5th PRG north of Munich, but he was then pursued by a P-51 of the 325th FG. Weber was able to outrun the Mustang. On the 3rd, Oberfeldwebel August Lübking of III./JG 7 claimed a B-17 from the Fifteenth Air Force. Another F-5, this time from the 7th PRG, fell to the guns of Oberfeldwebel Erich Büttner, a former *E.Kdo* 262 pilot, on 23 December. Again, P-51s were on the scene, and low-altitude air combat ensued, during which Büttner and Oberfeldwebel Albert Böckel, also of III. *Gruppe*, each claimed a Mustang.

The New Year was a portent of things to come. On New Year's Day, Unteroffizier Helmut Detjens of 10./JG 7 took off on his first operational flight against the enemy accompanied by his *Staffelkapitän*, the recently promoted Oberleutnant Joachim Weber. As he climbed, Detjens began to experience landing gear problems. Weber throttled back and flew a wide circle while instructing the young Unteroffizier to land. Weber recorded;

'Despite clear visibility, Detjens wanted me to lead him back to the airfield. Instructions from the control tower were quite clear, and Detjens was brought back over his own field. He, however, did not realise this. Unfortunately, Detjens was not equal to this situation. He flew over the field and made a forced-landing beyond owing to fuel shortage. He claimed that his fuel position had altered since landing was ordered and that he did not understand the position. The crash can be attributed to Detjens' inexperience.'

That same day, as B-17s from the Eighth Air Force's 1st Air Division (AD) returned from bombing German airfields in the Magdeburg area, 1Lt Franklin Young of the 4th FG, which was engaged in withdrawal escort for the bombers, intercepted the Me 262 flown by Leutnant Heinrich Lönnecker of 9./JG 7. He intercepted the fighter at an altitude of 1000 m, whereupon the jet nose-dived towards the earth and exploded southwest of Fassberg.

A lucky star seemed to shine on Unteroffizier Helmut Detjens. Having survived his accident on 1 January, exactly two weeks later, he was flying as part of a small formation of Me 262s from 9. and 11./JG 7 that joined the piston-engined fighters of JG 300 and JG 301 in engaging more than 600 B-17s and B-24s, and their escorts, despatched to bomb oil targets in northern Germany. Detjens was attacked by P-51s of the 353rd FG that were escorting the Liberators on their outward leg. It seems that his aircraft received fire from a P-51, which shot up the machine from port to starboard. Detjens was forced to pull up sharply and bail out. A fellow pilot from 9./JG 7, Unteroffizier Heinrich Wurm, was pursued by three P-51s at high speed and eventually crashed into a field from a height of just 15 m.

On either 14 or 17 January, Hauptmann Eder – since 25 November a recipient of the Oak Leaves to the Knight's Cross – claimed a B-17 shot down. Such victories were few and far between, however, and the early operational performance of JG 7 so far, hardly a great improvement over those of *E.Kdo* 262 (in fairness little more than a trials unit) and *Kommando Nowotny*, did not exactly produce the results that Galland had hoped for. But in any case, Galland's disappointment was academic, for with his relationship with Göring falling to an all-time low, the Reichsmarschall dismissed him as *General der Jagdflieger*, convinced he had become little more than an ineffective troublemaker. Simultaneous to Galland's dismissal, Steinhoff too was discharged from his command of JG 7. He later wrote;

'The order said neither where I should report nor whom I now came under. All it told me was, "Beat it, at the double – we don't need you anymore".'

Perhaps not surprisingly, Steinhoff's successor was the experienced Major Weissenberger. His imminent task would be to lead the *Geschwader* through its most intense phase of combat operations.

CHAPTER FIVE

PRODUCTION AND TRAINING

erhaps against the odds, more Me 262s were being built. The labour commitment was significant. On 31 December 1944, 28,766 'operatives', exclusive of personnel engaged on main jig construction and research, were employed in production, comprising 10,553 hands at Messerschmitt's Augsburg works and 7710 hands at Regensburg. A further 10,503 personnel were employed by main contractors and sub-contractors. Of the overall total, 48 per cent was categorised as 'productive' as opposed to 'unproductive', the former comprising hands working on component manufacture and sub- and main assembly, whilst the latter covered senior administrative personnel and their staffs, senior engineers and test hands, and personnel involved with raw materials.

According to a report prepared by Dipl.-Ing. Ludwig Bölkow, a senior aerodynamicist and engineer based at Messerschmitt Oberammergau, for a senior SS personnel officer in the Ministry of Propaganda and Public Enlightenment, by October 1944 a total of 265 aircraft had been produced, of which 30 had been destroyed in Allied air attacks. This figure was below the planned output, and with little prospect of any major improvement in conditions by the end of the year, it was forecast that production would total 130 in November and 200 in December.

Bölkow concluded that it would be impossible to improve things, and that considerable effort would be required to reach even a 'respectable' level by December. The principal challenges were the shortages of jigs and

A pilot from III./KG(J) 54 glances at the photographer from the wing of an Me 262A-1a at Neuburg/Donau in March 1945. The former bomber pilots of the *Gruppe* held the advantage of being familiar with twin-engined aircraft, but the jet was still a daunting challenge, especially when flying it in the interceptor role against heavily defended USAAF bomber formations and their fighter escorts. If he is about to fly a mission, this pilot will not thank the photographer – a shot like this, taken immediately before a flight, was considered an ill omen (*EN Archive*)

A civilian engineer starts the port-side Jumo 004 engine of what appears to be a freshly produced Me 262. The flame is as a result of leaking fuel pooling in the base of the engine cowling and igniting upon start-up. The Me 262 construction infrastructure was vast, employing more than 28,000 personnel at Augsburg and Regensburg, but bottlenecks and delays to parts and engines plagued production through to the end of the war (*EN Archive*)

tools, a persisting lack of skilled labour and what he saw as 'the bureaucracy of the RLM and the Todt Organisation'. This had an adverse effect on flight-testing and acceptance because of the large numbers of components which still had to be made by hand – a situation compounded by transport problems. The serious shortage of Junkers fitter personnel required for the reception and servicing of Jumo engines also presented Messerschmitt with a serious problem.

This view is lent credence in the opinions of Gerd Lindner, a Messerschmitt director, technician and former chief research test pilot at Lechfeld. According to a post-war Allied interrogation report, Lindner believed satisfactory levels of production 'were capable of attainment given a due degree of priority and general support for Messerschmitt from the various competent authorities. He further opined that the firm had created a unified production control and it was up to the *Rüstungsstab* [a government and SS task group] to follow suit, and to nominate a single authority with overriding powers to take the place of the numerous special and factory commissioners who had so far encumbered the scene'.

However, according to a summary based on Delivery Plan 227/1 of 15 December 1944 prepared by Messerschmitt's *Sonderausschuss* (Special Committee) F.2, total deliveries from the Augsburg plant of all types up to 30 November was 411 and from Regensburg 26, with all the aircraft from the latter plant being A-2a 'bombers'. The bulk – 124 aircraft – were A-1a interceptors, while seven A-2as had been modified as 'auxiliary reconnaissance' aircraft fitted with an SSK camera and two MK 108 cannon. By the end of the year, total output for all variants was planned to reach 637 aircraft.

As rates of production and the number of operational Me 262 units slowly expanded in late 1944 despite production difficulties and bottlenecks, so an efficient and structured training system became essential.

TRAINING

In November 1944, III. *Gruppe* of *Ergänzungs-Jagdgeschwader* (EJG) 2 had been formed from what remained of *E.Kdo* 262 at Lechfeld. The intention was to set up a dedicated Me 262 operational training unit which would be able to offer pilots converting to the jet a comprehensive and thorough training programme. Initially, about 50 pilots were assembled from both fighter and bomber units and fighter school staffs and a selection was made of promising new pilots who were about halfway through their operational fighter training pool syllabus. The new pilots in the training pools were given a pre-jet flying course which consisted of finishing their regular 20 hours' flying time in conventional fighter aircraft with the throttles fixed in one position to reproduce a technical problem found in flying in the Me 262, the throttles of which were not to be adjusted in flight at high altitudes.

Upon their arrival at Lechfeld, all pilots, both experienced and inexperienced, were given three days' theoretical instruction in the operation and functioning of jet engines, the features and flying qualities of the Me 262, as well as some practice in operating the controls in a wingless training model. This introduction was followed by a course at Landsberg in the operation of conventional twin-engined aircraft. Pupils were given five hours of flying time in the Bf 110 and Siebel Si 204, practising take-offs, landings, flight with the *Zielvorsatzgerät* 16 (radio course indicator), instrument flying and flying on one engine. Upon completion of the course, the pilots returned to III./EJG 2 at Lechfeld, where they were given one more day of theoretical instruction prior to commencing conversion onto the Me 262.

Practical instruction on the Me 262 began with half-a-day's exercise in starting and stopping the jet motors and taxiing. Flying instruction consisted of a total of nine take-offs as follows;

1. Thirty minutes of circuits with only two main fuel tanks full
2. Same.
3. One hour aerobatics and aerial manoeuvring.
4. Ditto.
5. One hour high-altitude flight to 9000 m.
6. One hour cross-country flight at 3600–4500 m.
7. One hour flying in two-aircraft *Rotte* element, first with an instructor and then with another student.
8. Same.
9. Gunnery practice, firing all four MK 108s at ground targets. First approach without firing and four other approaches firing.

If a two-seat Me 262B-1 was available, students had the opportunity of practising stalls with an instructor, as well as landings on only one jet and operating the landing gear with compressed air. Instrument flying in an Si 204 was also interspersed with the jet training.

This was considered to be the absolute minimum with which to qualify a pilot for operational readiness on the Me 262. However, such training was severely restricted due to the shortage of Me 262B-1s, and even by the end of January 1945, III./EJG 2 recorded only three such machines on strength.

The unit was helped by the successive appointments of experienced commanding officers, commencing with Hauptmann Horst Geyer, erstwhile commander of *E.Kdo 262*, then Oberleutnant Ernst Wörner (see Chapter 2), formerly *Staffelkapitän* of 10./EJG 2, who also filled the role of '*Umschulungsleiter*' (head of conversion training), and finally Oberstleutnant Heinz Bär.

Oberst Heinz Bär sits on the port wing of an Me 262 attached to III./EJG 2 at Lechfeld. One of the Luftwaffe's most able unit commanders and accomplished fighter pilots, Bär neverthless fell foul of Göring, who viewed him as troublesome, and he was assigned to oversee Me 262 training at Lechfeld in February 1945 as a result. For an officer decorated with the Swords to the Knight's Cross and some 200 victory claims, this was, in effect, a 'demotion' (*EN Archive*)

Bär was a redoubtable figure in the fighter arm, his service career stretching back to 1939. Concluding the campaign over Britain in the summer of 1940 with 17 confirmed victories, he then flew in the Soviet Union with JG 51, and within two months had chalked up a total of 60 kills. The award of the Knight's Cross came in July 1941, followed by the Oak Leaves in August, a month which saw him down six Soviet aircraft in one day.

Leaving Russia in 1942, Bär was given command of JG 77 in the Mediterranean, where he claimed a further 45 victories and gained the Swords to the Knight's Cross, despite contracting a punishing bout of malaria and being stricken by gastric ulcers. Ill and exhausted from operations, Bär returned to Germany for a period of convalescence, before embarking on a long stint as one of the foremost operational commanders in the Defence of the Reich. However, his well-known outspokenness caused Göring to 'demote' him, and Bär was subsequently posted to JG 1 as a *Staffelkapitän* and then *Gruppenkommandeur*, before moving on in mid-1944 to take over JG 3. By war's end, his victory list stood at 220.

Despite the application of Bär's energy and leadership, throughout December 1944, the number of pilots undergoing training with III./EJG 2 at Lechfeld increased dramatically in proportion to the size of the instructor cadre – a total of 135 trainee pilots for only 28 instructors, although the ratio of aircraft to pilots was even lower.

In addition to the bombing operations being conducted by KG 51, the pilots of some bomber *Gruppen* had commenced conversion training for flying the Me 262 as a fighter. This idea is believed to have originated with the bomber commander Generalmajor Dietrich Peltz, who had proposed converting units of IX. *Fliegerkorps*, which he had commanded until mid-October 1944, over to the jet interceptor. His rationale, which was supported by other senior 'bomber men', was based on the fact the bomber units, which, as a result of Germany's military predicament, had become largely redundant. This left a pool of available pilots with combat experience, trained on multi-engined aircraft and bad weather flying. Although Galland and his supporters objected to Peltz' proposals, Göring backed them, and conversion training commenced.

The first elements of a bomber *Geschwader* to convert over to the Me 262 in the fighter defence role, the *Stab* and I./KG 54 commenced training at Giebelstadt at the end of September 1944 with just three Me 262s and 56 pilots under Hauptmann Otfried Sehrt. With such odds, the *Geschwaderkommodore*, Oberstleutnant Volprecht Riedesel *Freiherr* zu Eisenbach, commenced training with only his most experienced pilots. At the beginning of October, the wing was redesignated KG(J) 54 ('J' denoting *'Jagd'* for fighter) and I. *Gruppe* received a two-seat Me 262B-1a trainer and six Fw 190s to further assist with conversion.

In November III./KG(J) 54 was joined by II. *Gruppe* in the training programme when it took on an Me 262B-1, three A-1as and four

An instructor leans against the fuselage of Me 262 'White 10' of III./EJG 2 at Lechfeld as another pilot sits in the cockpit familiarising himself with the jet interceptor's instruments in the autumn of 1944. Note the aircraft is fitted with 'Wikingerschiff' bomb racks. In the summer and autumn of 1944, student pilots would reach this point only after they had undergone a training programme on twin-engined aircraft as well as theoretical instruction on the jet engine. Later in the war, however, as the military situation became increasingly critical, training became correspondingly more hurried and rudimentary (*EN Archive*)

A relatively small number of dedicated two seat Me 262B-1a trainers were built, but there were too few and they arrived too late to really make an impact on the overall training effort. This aircraft, ??+ZM, made an emergency landing near Luzec nad Vltavou, 42 km north of Prague in Czechoslovakla, on 4 May 1945. It is believed to have been assigned to KG 51 and/or 4./KG(J) 54 (*EN Archive*)

Ar 96s at its base at Neuburg/Donau. I./KG(J) 54 also received four Ar 96s in mid-December, and these aircraft were used to practise formation flying in two-aircraft *Rotten* and four-aircraft *Schwärme*. However, training for both *Gruppen* was always plagued by a shortage of spares and J2 fuel, as well as destroyed and damaged ground-support equipment.

Freshly and probably insufficiently trained, pilots of I./KG(J) 54 did fly some sporadic operations in their jets against American reconnaissance Lightnings and bomber formations from the Fifteenth Air Force in December. On the 17th, six Me 262s mounted the *Geschwader*'s first ground-attack operation when they strafed American troops near Saint Vith in support of the German offensive in the Ardennes.

On 19 January, with pilots having received approximately six hours of individual familiarisation on the Me 262, 16 jets belonging to the *Stab* and I. *Gruppe* took off on the first of three formation exercises. Unhappily, however, on 26 January, Riedesel had to report to the headquarters of IX.(J) *Fliegerkorps* that all three exercises flown between 19–23 January had been dogged by technical problems and pilot errors which, in turn, had resulted in a number of abortive take-offs and crashes. Meanwhile, II./KG(J) 54 began forming up at Kitzingen.

In addition, in late November, a new training *Gruppe*, the *Ergänzungskampfgruppe* (J) (Erg.KGr.(J)) was formed from IV./KG 27 and based at Pilsen in order to commence fighter conversion training of former bomber pilots attached to units of IX.(J) *Fliegerkorps*, with KG 6, KG 27, KG 30 and KG 55 all shortly to be redesignated as 'KG(J)' units. The Erg.KGr.(J) was then expanded into two *Gruppen*, with I./Erg.KGr.(J) remaining at Pilsen under Hauptmann Walter Grasemann and II./Erg.KGr.(J), under Oberstleutnant Walter Junghans, being established at Neuburg.

A number of fighter pilots were assigned to these units to assist with training, including Knight's Cross-holder Major Diethelm von Eichel-Streiber, the former *Kommandeur* of III./JG 51 and I./JG 27, who was involved for a short period.

CHAPTER SIX

DAYLIGHT OPERATIONS PHASE 1

Me 262 jet bombers are readied for another operation over the Western Front on a cold day, probably at Hopsten, in December 1944 or January 1945. The white nose tips of 1./KG 51 are just visible (*EN Archive*)

I n late 1944, Generalmajor Peltz came up with another initiative. As commander of II. *Jagdkorps* since mid-October, he decided that the best way in which to offer support to the armoured thrust in the Ardennes was to neutralise Allied tactical air power where it was at its most vulnerable – on the ground. At the first suitable break in the weather, at dawn on 1 January 1945, German fighters from 33 *Gruppen* left their forward bases and headed in tight formation at low-level to attack several Allied airfields. Although surprise was achieved and moderate success gained at some targets, at others the results were nothing short of catastrophic.

As part of the attack force, 21 Me 262 bombers from I./KG 51, each carrying a pair of 250 kg bombs, struck at Eindhoven and Gilze-Rijen airfields in what was by far the largest effort mounted by the unit to date. Initially, things did not go well, for the aircraft of the *Gruppenkommandeur*, Major Heinz Unrau, and the *Staffelkapitän*, Oberleutnant Rudolf Abrahamczik, could not be started, so command was passed to Oberleutnant Haeffner of 2./KG 51, who recalled;

'Near Arnhem, 15 enemy fighters attacked us, but we managed to evade them. After approaching the target, we dived from 9000 m down to 1000 m and dropped our bombs. We then strafed the parked aircraft at low-level. I then flew once more over the field, taking photographs of the burning aeroplanes and wrecked hangars with my Robot camera. During the flight back to base I flew over Volkel airfield, where I saw at least 16 destroyed aircraft, taking more photographs. I landed safely at Hopsten at 0951 hrs.'

Throughout January, amidst generally poor weather, I./KG 51 continued to carry out regular nuisance attacks on Allied armour, vehicles and troops over the Alsace and the French–German border area further to the south.

The targets for I./KG 51 on 13 January were enemy troop concentrations in the Hagenauer Forest. The *Gruppe* was in the air during the early afternoon, and it made bomb and cannon-strafing attacks. Four Me 262s were lost, the first flown by Unteroffizier Alfred Färber of 1./KG 51, who was shot down by a P-51 of the 55th FG. As he circled Giebelstadt airfield, the American pilot, 1Lt Walter J Konantz, 'caught him easily as he was in a medium turn and got a long burst into him from 200 yards. He caught fire near the port jet unit and made a diving turn straight into the ground about half-a-mile from the aerodrome. He exploded with a big flash of flame when he hit'.

In a typical mission for the period, the next morning Oberleutnant Haeffner, accompanied by Leutnant Wilhelm Batel and Oberfeldwebel Hermann Wieczorek, took off to attack targets near Durrenbach. Their Me 262A-2as were each loaded with a pair of 250 kg bombs and drop tanks. Despite light AA fire and the presence of enemy fighters in the target area, the jets dropped their ordnance on American tank columns, with hits being observed.

As January drew to a close, Oberstleutnant Schenck handed command of KG 51 to Oberstleutnant Rudolf Hallensleben and took up the appointment of *Inspizient für Strahlflugzeuge* (Inspector of Jet Aircraft) in the RLM. At the end of the month I./KG 51 had around 50 Me 262s operational and II./KG 51 had 23. Worryingly, however, attrition due to combat and non-combat casualties was taking its toll – the total strength of I. and II./KG 51 at the end of January was equal to the strength of I. *Gruppe* alone at the end of November.

Also intending to support German ground forces over the Western Front were small numbers of Me 262 reconnaissance aircraft, but in reality their tactical value at this stage remained of little consequence, and very few such machines had been delivered by Messerschmitt. Hauptmann Karl-Heinz Wilke had been appointed *Kommandeur* of NAGr. 1, which was intended as a new *Gruppe*, with, a few days later, Oberleutnant Wilhelm Knoll being appointed as *Kapitän* of 1. *Staffel*, which was to be formed from elements of 1./F 121.

However, the equipping process proved to be extremely slow. By 19 January, the *Gruppe* reported just two pilots and no aircraft on strength. The *Stab*, 1. and 2./NAGr. 1 were at Herzogenaurach, and after a few days

Tense expressions on the faces of pilots of I./KG 51 at Hopsten reflect the deteriorating military situation confronting Germany in the late autumn of 1944. At far right is *Gruppenkommandeur*, Major Heinz Unrau, while from left to right are Oberfeldwebel Erich Kaiser of 1. *Staffel*, Oberleutnante Klein and Kühn (both signals officers), Oberleutnant Ludwig Albersmeyer (operations officer) and Hauptmann Rudolf Abrahamczik, *Kapitän* of 2./KG 51 (*EN Archive*)

the *Stab* had a solitary Me 262 and four Bf 110s on strength, but the two *Staffeln* remained with neither aircraft nor pilots. Eventually, around ten pilots assembled at Herzogenaurach for familiarisation on the jet.

They were quickly sent on a high-altitude adjustment course at a remote ski hut on the *Zugspitze*. This was followed by a week of theoretical instruction on the construction and functioning of jet engines at Schwabstadtl. Finally, at the beginning of February, practical instruction commenced at Lechfeld. This would last six weeks, and would include take-offs, circuits, high-altitude flights, ferry flights, formation flying, blind-flying and RATO starts. By 17 January, *Stab*/NAGr. 1 reported two jets on strength.

Kdo. Panther, operating under 5. *Jagddivision*, flew reconnaissance missions over the Hagenau-Strasbourg area during mid-January. On the 20th, Braunegg's *Kommando* was incorporated into 2./NAGr. 6, with Braunegg taking over command. Major Friedrich Heinz Schultze, from the staff of the *General der Aufklärer*, took overall command of the *Gruppe* from Major Hermann Harbig, while Oberleutnant Georg Keck was *Kapitän* of 1./NAGr. 6. Schultze held a keen interest in the possibilities offered by high-speed, jet-powered reconnaissance aircraft and had studied the reports of the experiences of the Ar 234-equipped *Kdo. Götz* as well as the periodic reports of Braunegg, which had been prepared for his immediate superior, Generalmajor von Barsewisch. By the end of the month, *Kommando Braunegg*/2.NAGr. 6 had five Me 262s on strength.

To the east, at Brandenburg-Briest, the handful of pilots assigned to JG 7 prepared to go into action. As *Kommandeur* of III. *Gruppe*, Major Rudolf Sinner arrived on 24 January to take over from Major Erich Hohagen, who was effectively dismissed by Weissenberger. Sinner, a veteran of the North African, Mediterranean and Balkan theatres, where he had flown Bf 109s with JG 27, cautiously recognised the combat potential of the Me 262 and its suitability for aerial defence;

'We could attack heavily defended and escorted bomber formations with a considerable chance of success and less risk than was the case with piston fighters. Alongside this, with repeated individual attacks by smaller numbers of combat-experienced pilots in Me 262s, we could seriously harass and confuse strong groups of enemy escort fighters and divert them from their planned defence of the bombers.

'However, there were a number of disadvantages – flight duration was shorter and more dependent on altitude than a piston fighter. It was defenceless during take-off and landing and the powerplants were more likely to suffer disturbance and had a shorter life than piston engines. Also, the demands upon airfield size, ground support, engineering, flight safety and tactical management were greater and not adequately attended to. In summary, due to its advantages, the Me 262 was, despite these disadvantages, essentially better-suited to the defence of the Reich than our piston-engined fighters of the time. For field operations, it was less well-suited.'

Hauptmann Herward Braunegg, *Staffelkapitän* of 2./NAGr. 6, applies the accelerator from the driver's seat of a bogged-down staff car somewhere on the Western Front in early 1945. Leutnant F W Schlüter provides some assistance at the back, watched by Oberleutnant Erich Weiss and Dr Wolfgang Riese (*EN Archive*)

Combat sorties seem to have been sporadic at this time and as with the previous month, the isolated victories were marred by losses. The paucity in operations may have been due to the fact that the Chief of the Luftwaffe Operations Staff had to give 'permission' to III./JG 7 to engage enemy reconnaissance aircraft and fighters. It seems the Me 262 was still too precious a resource to lose in the testing battle against Allied bombers.

During the first weeks of 1945, however, some highly capable fighter pilots were assigned to command positions with JG 7. Succeeding Weissenberger as leader of I./JG 7 was Major Erich Rudorffer, who had flown with JG 2 as an NCO in the French campaign of May 1940. His subsequent service career was impressive to say the least. He was awarded the Knight's Cross a year later for his 19 victories. Rudorffer proved to be a potent adversary against the Western Allies, shooting down two Spitfires in one day over Dieppe in August 1942. In November of that year, he was appointed *Staffelkapitän* of 6./JG 2 and his unit moved to Tunisia, where he shot down eight British aircraft in 32 minutes on 9 February 1943. Six days later, in a remarkable feat, seven more enemy aircraft fell to his guns.

Rudorffer then took command of II./JG 2, but returned to France in April 1943. Subsequently, he was appointed *Kommandeur* of IV. and then II./JG 54. On one occasion over the Soviet Union, Rudorffer claimed 13 Soviet machines shot down in 17 minutes. The Oak Leaves to the Knight's Cross followed on 11 April 1944 when his tally stood at 134 victories. After several more incidents of multiple 'kills' in one day over the Eastern Front, he was awarded the Swords to Knight's Cross upon his 212th victory on 26 January 1945 – the 126th such recipient.

By the time he reached JG 7, Rudorffer had shot down 136 enemy aircraft on the Eastern Front. He would end the war having clocked up more than 1000 missions, involving more than 300 encounters with the enemy that resulted in ten four-engined bombers destroyed. Bailing out on no fewer than nine occasions, Rudorffer was himself shot down 16 times.

Leutnant Rudolf Rademacher was another JG 54 veteran who had scored 90 victories flying under Major Walter Nowotny in the Soviet Union before serving as a fighter instructor. He had been seriously wounded while flying an Fw 190 in a mission against American heavy bombers on 18 September 1944 and was awarded the Knight's Cross on 30 September for 81 victories. Recovered from his wounds, Rademacher joined 11./JG 7 on 30 January 1945.

Thus, with its 'backbone' of accomplished aces such as Weissenberger, Eder, Sinner, Rudorffer and Rademacher, JG 7 was blessed with a core of experienced pilots with which to lead its operations against the Allied air forces.

The same could not be said for the 'conversion unit', KG(J) 54, although on 14 January Oberstleutnant Riedesel was awarded the Oak Leaves to his Knight's Cross in recognition of his service as the *Geschwader*'s *Kommodore* since 1943 and his 500 operational missions. As for his *Geschwader*, on 5 January II. *Gruppe* commenced forming up as an interceptor unit at Gardelegen, transferring to Kitzingen on the 13th, while I./KG(J) 54 was fully equipped with Me 262s at Giebelstadt, but usually at only around 50 per cent readiness/serviceability. The *Gruppe* was plagued by faults with its aircraft, accidents and crashes. Conditions at Giebelstadt were made

OPPOSITE
Exiled aces. From early March 1945, Generalleutnant Adolf Galland, the former *General der Jagdflieger*, was once again the commander of a small fighter unit. From the beginning of the following month, his JV 44 flew interceptor missions in the Me 262 mainly against US tactical air forces attacking targets in southern Germany and Austria. Galland is seen here at left at the unit's base at Munich-Riem accompanied by Oberst Günther Lützow, a highly respected Luftwaffe unit commander who had led the protest against Göring over the Reichsmarschall's treatment of Galland. Both men found flying the Me 262 challenging (*EN Archive*)

Me 262A-1a 'White 5' of 11./JG 7 is
serviced close to what appears to be a
bomb crater at Brandenburg-Briest in late
January or early February 1945. By this
stage of the war, the jet airfields were
targeted regularly by USAAF heavy
bombers. Of conditions at Munich-Riem,
the base of JV 44 , Generalleutnant Adolf
Galland commented that the 'American
"Jabos" would even attack a stray dog'
(*EN Archive*)

harder by regular strafing attacks conducted by USAAF Mustangs that also
affected training (see Chapter 5).

Unlike Sinner of III./JG 7, Riedesel and his *Gruppenkommandeur*,
Hauptmann Sehrt, were not so enthused about the Me 262. They knew
that it was a priority for their pilots to master formation flying, but they
found this difficult given the high speed of the jet. Furthermore, take-off and
assembly of a *Gruppe* of Me 262s into battle formation took a considerable
amount of time. The erstwhile bomber pilots also found that the Jumo 004
turbines lacked sufficient sensitivity to be able to make quick manoeuvres.
This meant that wide, slow turns had to be flown which resulted in a loss of
time, and was not acceptable in combat conditions. It was this factor which
probably contributed to the aforementioned loss of I./KG 51's Unteroffizier
Färber to the P-51 of 1Lt Konantz of the 55th FG on 13 January.

Meanwhile, during January, as JG 7 prepared to defend the skies over
Berlin, Generalleutnant Adolf Galland left the confines of an apartment
in the city where he had been languishing under house arrest and drove
to Göring's country estate at Carinhall to the northeast of
the capital. As he arrived, he could hear the sound of artillery
thundering away to the east as the Red Army pressed home its
winter offensive across the Oder.

Galland found the Reichsmarschall to be in an uncompromising
mood. Göring maintained that his former Fighter General had
let him down, and that the fighter arm needed more disciplined
management. In the meantime, however, Göring would allow
Galland one last chance to prove that the Me 262 should be used
exclusively as a fighter, and the only way to do that was by trial
in combat.

Göring had prepared the ground for the establishment of a *Staffel*-
strength unit to be placed under Galland's personal command. He
would have some autonomy, but he would have to obtain his own
aircraft and pilots. He would also be assigned Oberst Johannes
Steinhoff and another dismissed fighter commander, Oberst
Günther Lützow, who had led the clique of discontented officers in
their complaints against Göring and his leadership style. Galland
thanked the Reichsmarschall and returned to Berlin to start work.

In early February the Allies prepared to drive on the Rhine. Their advance would be across a front of 400 km, from the Swiss border, across eastern France, Luxembourg, Belgium and into the Netherlands. In the north, the forces of Bradley and Montgomery would mount a series of assaults on the great river and attempt exploitation of the German defences.

On the 2nd no fewer than 25 Me 262s from I./KG 51 were detailed to strike against troops of the French First Army in the Colmar area, east of the Vosges, in support of 19. *Armee*. The *Gruppe* reported 22 aircraft over the target and explosions at Ostheim, north of Colmar, together with hits on vehicle concentrations on the northern edge of the Colmar Forest. Leutnant Hubert Lange of 1./KG 51 was assigned the railway station at Ostheim as a target, but as he approached the area he was fired upon by AA batteries. Nevertheless, he was able to carry out a gliding attack and dropped his bomb from 1600 m, observing that it hit the area between the station and the town. Lange returned to Giebelstadt safely.

Once again, Oberleutnant Heinrich Haeffner was flying:

'I was allocated a new Me 262, and took off to attack Colmar at 1321 hrs. Approaching the target, I again met a large number of enemy bomber formations with strong fighter escort heading for the Reich. As on earlier occasions, I flew towards the fighters and fired several bursts at them. The fighters immediately jettisoned their tanks, expecting an attack. I climbed away steeply, the fighters being unable to follow. Having dropped my bombs on Colmar, I touched down at Giebelstadt at 1420 hours. The groundcrew quickly refuelled and rearmed my aircraft with bombs.'

Early February was to prove a busy time for both I. and II./KG 51, the latter *Gruppe* under the command of Major Martin Vetter. Me 262s of 5./KG 51 flew operations against a supply dump at Maastricht, 900 m north of the railway bridge, on the 3rd. This was, however, viewed as an 'alternative target'. On the 4th, a single jet from KG 51 dropped two SC 250 bombs in the Barr area, north of Schlettstadt, during a weather reconnaissance flight, but results were not observed. The next day, 3. *Jagddivision* instructed that KG 51 was to be used in ways 'which are decisive and promise success' – perhaps an indication that results were not viewed as being entirely acceptable.

By 14 February, British and Canadian forces were approaching the south bank of the Rhine opposite the fortified town of Kleve, leading KG 51 to fly a total of 55 sorties against Allied ground targets in the area during the day. Me 262s worked in cooperation with Ar 234s from KG 76 in an early morning strike on the town.

The units reported 35 aircraft over the target between 0755 hrs and 0916 hrs, of which 13 were from KG 51. Four Me 262s made it as far as the target, while one broke off due to a technical problem. Leutnant Dieter Mundt of 6./KG 51 dropped a single SD 250 from his Me 262A-1a on his assigned target at Zyfflich, northwest of Kranenburg, nine kilometres west of Kleve, having avoided an encounter with a formation of P-51s in the target area, as well as heavy AA fire.

Unteroffizier Martin Golde, also of 6. *Staffel*, was briefed to attack troop assembly points in the same area, but instead struck at Nijmegen as an alternative target, making a glide attack from 2000 m. He landed safely at Essen-Mühlheim after a 29-minute sortie, and his aircraft was rearmed and refuelled in readiness for a second mission, this time to Kranenburg. However, as he neared the target, he spotted some Tempest Vs and so turned for the secondary target at Nijmegen, which he attacked in a glide from 1500 m. He returned to Essen 33 minutes later.

The *Geschwader* maintained a steady pace of operations against the Kleve area, as well as targeting armour of the US First and Ninth Armies as they began a heavy attack along the Roer, especially in the Jülich area. The Me 262s also dropped fragmentation bomb containers over American troop concentrations in the Linnich–Düren area.

The Me 262 reconnaissance force was also active in early February, with NAGr. 6 having been ordered to transfer to Münster-Handorf and Essen-Mühlheim for operations over the Western Front. Three Me 262s from 2./NAGr. 6 (formerly *Kdo. Panther*) flew photo-reconnaissance sorties in the Roermond area where the British Second Army was engaged against forces of the German *Heeresgruppe* H, as well to the west of the Scheldt, but all were unsuccessful owing to the bad weather. Another two Me 262s from NAGr. 6 flew road reconnaissance in the Strasbourg–Schlettstadt–Colmar area, but again this was only partially successful due to the weather.

On 10 February, 2./NAGr. 6 despatched two Me 262s on a photo-reconnaissance mission of the Zabern–Strasbourg area, while KG 51 also sent one of its jets on a similar mission over the same region. On the 14th, an advance detachment of 1./NAGr. 6 arrived at Essen-Mühlheim, and two jets from the unit flew photo-reconnaissance, one in the Drusenheim–Hagenau–Saarunio–-Saarburg–Wassenheim area and the other in the Hagenau–Bischweiler–Brumath–Strasbourg–Erstein area and west of the Rhine at Plosheim. The next day, NAGr. 6 mounted four operations, with two jets being sent on reconnaissance to Zabern–Saarburg–Ingweiler, while another conducted reconnaissance west of the Rhine. Another pair of Me 262s flew 'road patrols' over the Zabern–Saint-Avold–Ingweiler area and a single aircraft flew an armed reconnaissance to the Hagenau–Zabern–Strasbourg area.

Operations continued on 16 and 17 February, with an Me 262 from NAGr. 6 flying a photo-reconnaissance sortie in the Strasbourg–Habern–Ingweiler–Hagenau–Drusenheim area on the first day, while another covered Drusenheim–Hagenau–Saarunion–Salzbergen–Zabern–Strasbourg on the 17th, although it was forced to break off the flight due to bad weather.

On 20 February, 1./NAGr. 6 reported the loss of a reconnaissance aircraft, which was described in a report as an 'Me 262A-4'. This was a proposed Augsburg-built reconnaissance version of the Me 262. Then, on the 21st, Oberleutnant Knoll, *Staffelkapitän* of 1./NAGr. 1, which was converting to the jet, perished when his Me 262A-1a/U3 crashed southwest of Landsberg-am-Lech. He had been on a familiarisation ferry flight when, southeast of Landsberg, he noticed a pair of P-51s. Using his speed advantage, Knoll climbed to the same height as the American fighters and manoeuvred in behind them. Just before he got into a position to open fire, the P-51s broke to the left and right and quickly turned behind him to open fire, shooting him down. Following the death of Knoll, Hauptmann Friedrich Dünkel was appointed as the new commander of 1./NAGr. 1.

Pilots from all the Me 262 units were still having to contend with hazardous quirks of the jet, and accidents often resulted in the loss of a valuable aircraft. In the five days between 2–6 February, three Me 262s of JG 7 were lost or damaged due to accidents or engine fires – an increasingly common occurrence. Major Ludwig Grözinger of 11./JG 7 crashed near Lechfeld as a result of the same problem on the 11th. Grözinger was a former bomber pilot who had flown He 111s with KG 53 over England in 1940 and on the Eastern Front, where he was appointed *Staffelkapitän* of 3./KG 53 and later led IV./KG 53. During his time fighting Soviet forces, Grözinger had made some 80 successful bombing attacks on railway stations and had been awarded the Knight's Cross in November 1942.

Another such incident is recorded as taking place on the morning of 17 February, shortly after a pilot (probably Oberfeldwebel Hans Clausen) of III./JG 7 took off. The pilot later reported;

'I took off in "Green 2" at about 0902 hrs for a workshop test flight. During a *"Tornadoanflug"* [an approach using *'Tornado'*, an experimental direction beacon system] from Burg, after about ten minutes of flying time, the right turbine suddenly cut out, but was restarted and remained normal. Upon returning to the field, I had to overshoot due to an obstruction (motor vehicle).

'After climbing and orbiting the field I lowered the undercarriage again and found that the electrical indicator for the right mainwheel was not functioning. I turned on the compressed air bottle to operate the undercarriage. In spite of this, the indicator still did not register. I asked Control over the R/T if my undercarriage was down, and received the reply, "Turn over the tower". Then I suddenly noticed that the temperature of the right engine had risen to 700 degrees and that flames were coming from the engine with a loud hissing noise. Therefore, in order to cool the engine down, I throttled the right engine back. The engine stopped with a loud report. The aircraft yawed to the right and crashed in a young pine tree plantation in the Fohrde area after a dive at an angle of about 50 degrees.'

By early February, during the hours of daylight, the airspace over Germany had become an aerial 'battleground' between the Luftwaffe and Allied air forces. Since the autumn of 1944, the RAF had joined the USAAF in bombing Germany by day, and the first half of December had seen 136 pilots lost in home defence operations. But still III./JG 7 had not declared itself fully ready for operations.

On the 3rd, however, one of a range of targets for the USAAF were the marshalling yards at Berlin-Tempelhof. A total of 116 Liberators of the 2nd AD reached the target, but not before a small force of Me 262s from JG 7 had made its mark. Leutnant Rademacher claimed two 'B-17s' shot down, although it is more likely that these aircraft were B-24s. Oberleutnant Joachim Weber of 9./JG 7 and Oberleutnante Günther Wegmann and Karl Schnörrer of 11./JG 7 claimed one *'Viermot'* ('four-motor' – Allied four-engined bomber) each. Hauptmann Eder, leading 11./JG 7, is believed to have shot down two P-47s, while Unteroffizier Anton Schöppler claimed a P-51. The USAAF lost 23 B-17s, two B-24s and seven P-51s during the raid that day, the only claim against a jet being made by a Mustang pilot of the 364th FG who claimed to have damaged an Me 262 south of Gardelegen.

By 9 February I./JG 7 had just 12 aircraft on strength, and that same day Göring instructed that in order to reinforce the *Geschwader*, two Me 262 *Industrieschwärme* (factory defence flights) were to be disbanded and their personnel and aircraft transferred to JG 7. The 9th also saw the Eighth Air Force return to northern and central Germany, this time striking at oil, transport and airfield targets including Magdeburg, Lützkendorf and Paderborn. In the Berlin area, a few Me 262s from III./JG 7 attacked B-17s, with Rademacher claiming two shot down and Eder and Wegmann being credited with one each. Schnörrer claimed a P-51. But these were pinpricks against overwhelming force.

Three days later, on the 12th, III./JG 7 finally declared itself fully operational with 50 aircraft to conform to a deadline set by Göring. On the 14th the USAAF sent another large raid comprised of nearly 1300 B-17s and B-24s, escorted by 881 fighters, to 17 assorted targets including Dresden, Prague, Brüx, Pilsen, Chemnitz and Magdeburg. Some bombers were forced to return early and were intercepted by several Me 262s from I. *Gruppe* and 11./JG 7. Once again it was Rademacher and Schöppler who accounted for a bomber each and Unteroffizier Günther Engler, who had joined JG 7 from JG 3, was also credited with the destruction of one. The pilot of an Me 262 of the *Geschwader* was forced to bail out, having been attacked by the fighter escort.

At least three pilots from 9./JG 7 led by *Staffelkapitän*, Hauptmann Eder, were scrambled from Parchim on 17 February to intercept what were probably RAF bombers operating in daylight against the Ruhr. Eder was accompanied by another Knight's Cross-holder, Oberfeldwebel Hermann Büchner, and Oberfeldwebel Helmut Zander. The small formation of Me 262s sighted the bombers south of Bremen and the Luftwaffe pilots prepared to make an attack on the formation from the rear. As they did so, they were greeted by massed defensive fire from the enemy air gunners. Eder's Me 262 was hit and he was forced to bail out, suffering head injuries and a broken leg as a result.

As Oberfeldwebel Büchner explained to this author:

'The Me 262 reached us too late, though it was years ahead of its time from the point of view of its technology. Of course, there were shortcomings, but with more time and sufficient operational experience, these could have been eliminated. The main problem was that the crews had to work out new methods of attack and had to learn how to manage at such high speed. In an attack, firing time was reduced for we reached the target ridiculously fast. I accounted for most of my claims by basically approaching from the rear.

'Of course, you had to fly through the escort. This was somewhat more difficult with the Fw 190, but was no problem with the Me 262. With a sufficient number of Me 262s deployed, the escort fighters had no chance of preventing an Me 262 from making its attack. Attack began at a distance of 500 m; one had to overcome one's basic instincts and get through the defensive fire of the bomber. It was very important to make the target the tail-gunner's turret, just where you made out the muzzle flash and smoke of the machine guns. If the rear gunner had been taken out, success was much more certain. And when the R4M rocket [see Chapter 7] was introduced, the successes were even greater.'

On 22 February the Allied air forces launched Operation *Clarion*, a major bombing offensive specifically aimed at knocking out the German transport and communications system. Nearly 9000 aircraft, flying from bases in England, France, Holland, Belgium and Italy, targeted railways, bridges, ports and roads. The day may have seen the first 'maximum effort' on the part of JG 7, which utilised all of its available aircraft. In its Daily Situation Report, the OKL Operations Staff recorded;

'Thirty-four Me 262s of JG 7 took off, but were not able to engage the heavy bombers as they were immediately involved in intensive actions with enemy fighters. Only five enemy aircraft were shot down.'

OKL's figure is at odds with the claims made by its pilots. Oberleutnant Wegmann, now leading 11./JG 7 following Eder's demise, claimed a P-51, while Gefreiter Hermann Notter of the *Geschwader Stab* claimed two B-17s, following which he was forced to belly-land near Stade. Buchner shot down a P-51 of the 364th FG. I./JG 7 was operational, but only two machines managed to take off, that of the *Staffelkapitän* of 3./JG 7, Oberleutnant Hans-Peter Waldmann, and his wingman, Oberfähnrich Günther Schrey. Waldmann claimed two P-51s around midday near Oschersleben during a 66-minute sortie.

This combat was not without loss to JG 7, as was increasingly the case. Oberfeldwebel Helmut Baudach of 10. *Staffel*, a veteran of E.*Kdo* 262 and *Kdo. Nowotny*, struck his head against his aircraft's tail as he bailed out not far from Schönewald. He survived the incident, but died a few days later – it was another heavy blow to the unit, and meant the loss of an experienced jet pilot the Luftwaffe could ill afford. Oberfeldwebel Heinz-Berthold Mattuschka of 11./JG 7 escaped with his life when he also bailed out of his jet fighter near Hagenow.

Some 348 B-17s of the Eighth Air Force's 1st AD struck at two oil refineries at Hamburg on the 24th, and as they did so, 10. and 11./JG 7 attempted to intercept in the airspace between the city and Lüneburg. Despite the fact that the P-51 escort successfully screened the formation from attack, Rademacher put in a claim for a Flying Fortress destroyed and Weber for a Mustang. Three days later Rademacher struck again, raising his personal tally to 90 victories when he brought down a B-24 in the Halle-Leipzig area – one of two lost from the 314 Liberators of the 2nd AD sent to bomb the Halle marshalling yards.

February 1945 had seen 25 Me 262s delivered to I./JG 7, ten to II./JG 7 and seven to III./JG 7. This was out of a total of 212 jets squeezed from the factories, with a further 12 repaired. Curiously, the 'winning' unit in terms of taking delivery of new machines was not JG 7 – which was tasked with defending the critical area around the German capital – but rather KG(J) 54. This may have been attributable to the measure of influence that Generalmajor Peltz exerted. Whatever the case, JG 7 would need every single pilot and every single aircraft it could acquire, for the coming month would test the unit's mettle to its limit.

Me 262A-1as of III./KG(J) 54 taxi out for what was probably a training flight at Neuburg/Donau in March 1945. A member of the groundcrew is visible standing on the port wing root of the lead Me 262 in the centre foreground, guiding the pilot so as to avoid any surface debris. This aircraft is B3+GR, believed to be flown by instructor pilot Oberfeldwebel Friedrich Gentsch of 7./ KG(J) 54. The *Gruppe* was still undergoing operational training at this time (*EN Archive*)

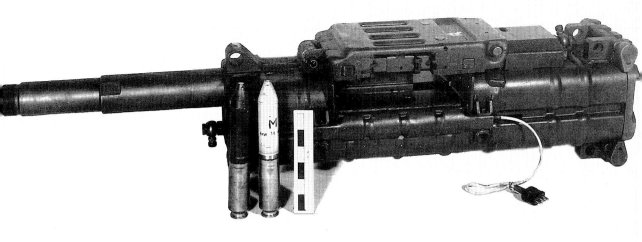

CHAPTER SEVEN

WEAPONRY

The Me 262A-1a carried four air-cooled, belt-fed, 30 mm MK 108 cannon in its nose. Seen here positioned upright next to the cannon are an incendiary shell (at left) and a *Minengeschoss* (mine shell) marked with an 'M'. Such ammunition was used, respectively, to cause fire in fuel tanks and blast effect within a bomber's fuselage. In the 'M' shell the upper part of the round contained the fuse, detonator, booster, explosive and closing plug. Also seen is the wire to which was attached the firing solenoid (*Author Collection*)

The standard armament for the Me 262 interceptor, bomber and reconnaissance aircraft was the 30 mm Rheinmetall-Borsig MK 108 cannon. The interceptor prototypes and A-1a production variant 'drove' the armament philosophy in as much as the MK 108 was a high-calibre cannon, which was dubbed the 'pneumatic hammer' by the Luftwaffe, earning a fearsome reputation amongst Allied bomber crews. Two types of shells could be used – the 30 mm high-explosive tracer type 'M' shell designed to cause blast effect, and the 30 mm high-explosive incendiary shell. Both were capable of inflicting considerable damage on a large, four-engined enemy bomber.

The MK 108 was a blow-back operated, rear-seared, belt-fed weapon, using electric ignition and being charged and triggered by compressed air. A total of 60 rounds was fed by means of a disintegrating belt from an ammunition canister mounted above the gun. The weapon's advantage lay in its simplicity and economic process of manufacture, the greater part of its components consisting of pressed sheet metal stampings.

With the advent of massed American daylight bomber formations fielding concentrated defensive firepower, the need arose for a heavy calibre gun with which a German pilot could expend the least amount of ammunition, score a kill in the shortest possible time and yet stay beyond the range of the defensive guns. It was a virtually impossible requirement, and yet the MK 108 did achieve this.

Four MK 108s were fitted into the nose of the Me 262A-1a, while the A-2a had two cannon in the lower weapon position, with the upper gun ports being faired over. Reconnaissance variants were usually fitted with a single weapon off-set in the upper nose, the barrel of the cannon protruding slightly on the starboard side.

Generalleutnant Adolf Galland recalled the gun being installed in the Me 262;

'Firstly, in terms of construction, it was extraordinarily easy to install four MK 108s into the aircraft. Secondly, it was good to have a gun which solved all our problems; that is to say a gun which had a rapid rate of fire and great destructive effect, although there was the disadvantage of an insufficiently flat trajectory. There were snags. The guns were not that much good when you were banking because the centrifugal forces arising from such a manoeuvre ripped the belts. But these teething troubles were easily sorted out by a well-trained groundcrew.'

One Me 262 was fitted with six MK 108s to become probably the only A-1a/U5 prototype. An extension to the nose accommodated the additional cannon. In March 1945 the aircraft was assigned to III./EJG 2 at Lechfeld, but when that unit's *Kommandeur*, Oberstleutnant Heinz Bär, was transferred to JV 44 in late April, he took the aircraft with him to the unit's base at Munich-Riem. It is believed that Bär flew the A-1a/U5 operationally on 27 April when he engaged USAAF fighters and shot at least one down.

AIR-TO-AIR BOMBING

The idea of using the Me 262 in the air-to-air bombing role originated with Oberst Berndt von Brauchitsch, Göring's Chief Adjutant. Brauchitsch believed that such tactics could break up a tight-flying enemy bomber formation, thus breaking down the density of its combined defensive firepower and thereby producing favourable conditions for attack by German fighters. Although this might seem a somewhat implausible proposition, Brauchitsch believed that the jet's superior speed would overcome the problem of the fighter escort, and that damage could be inflicted with jettisonable weapons containers loaded with semi-armour-piercing bombs equipped with barometric fuses designed to produce maximum blast effect.

Early in January 1945, four Me 262s were delivered to *Kdo. Stamp*, an experimental air-to-air bombing unit based at Lärz. The unit was led by Knight's Cross-holder Major Gerhard Stamp, a former Ju 88 bomber pilot who pioneered *Wilde Sau* (Wild Boar) single-seat nightfighter operations, before taking command of I./JG 300, which provided high-altitude cover for heavily-armoured Fw 190-equipped *Sturmgruppen* operating in the defence of the Reich.

Stamp planned to use four Me 262s to make an attack on an enemy formation, with each aircraft initially carrying one bomb. The jets would fly echeloned back 10–15 degrees in a loose line astern formation, with about 28 m between each aircraft. They were to fly next to the bomber formation and at the same altitude, assign targets, then make their approach from the front and some 915 m above the formation in order to avoid contact with any enemy fighter escort.

Each Me 262 attached to the *Kommando* was marked with a coloured stripe on the nose that slanted downward towards the front at an angle of 16 degrees below the horizontal. At the correct range (about 2740 m) from which the pilot would commence his attack dive, it was intended that he would use the stripe to line up the formation. The four-degree differential between the 20-degree attack angle and the 16-degree stripe was compensated by the time it took to go into the dive at a speed of 750–800 kph. At a distance of 550 m, the bombs would be released, after which the Me 262s broke away by 'split-essing' or climbing over the bomber formation, before returning to base.

Ordnance types included the AB 500 container loaded with either 25 SD 15 Zt semi armour-piercing bombs equipped with time fuses or 84 SD 3s. Another variation was to load the AB 500 with 4000 *Brandtaschen* (incendiary pellets) and enough explosive to scatter the pellets with sufficient velocity – similar to that of a massive shotgun blast – in order to penetrate the skin of a bomber.

Several test flights with barometric fuses were carried out over the Müritz See throughout January 1945, but the venture proved unfeasible. For example, it was found that after a canister had opened, bombs hit each other and detonated too quickly, the resultant blast severely damaging the carrier aircraft.

Despite the best efforts of its five or so pilots, *Kdo. Stamp* failed in its task. On 3 February, Generalmajor Eckhard Christian, the Chief of the Luftwaffe Operations Staff, recommended to Brauchitsch that *Kdo. Stamp* be disbanded 'at once'.

'The essential objections', Christian wrote, 'are that the enemy will immediately prevent bomb-dropping by using fighter escort at an even higher altitude in addition to the normal escort. By exploiting the necessarily long bombing run, enemy fighters using a 1000 m altitude advantage have a clear chance of shooting down even jet aircraft. The present type of enemy formation offers the least favourable conditions for breaking up a formation.

'By and large the results of Major Stamp's experiment are still wide open. The procedures are still uncertain and have not been tested tactically. These considerations lead to the belief that, in spite of the improved technical position, no lasting success is to be expected. In the present situation, the necessary tests, personnel adjustments, material expenditure etc., do not appear justified.

'In order to carry out the *Führer*'s demands, the immediate need is to assemble all Me 262s for operation as quickly as possible. Six Me 262s were assigned to *Kdo. Stamp*, four have been allocated. It does not appear justifiable to divert aircraft of this type for an experiment which will not produce conclusive results in a short time period. The *Luftwaffenführungsstab* proposes that Major Stamp's project is dropped at once.'

Shortly after, *Kdo. Stamp*'s aircraft and personnel were integrated into JG 7, becoming known as the *Stabsstaffel* JG 7.

WERFER-GRANATE 21 AIR-TO-AIR MORTAR

The 21 cm *Nebelwerfer* 42 mortar was designed as an infantry weapon for use in ground warfare. The original concept for airborne employment was to install the spin-stabilised mortars under the wings of Fw 190s for use as an air-to-air weapon against formations of four-engined bombers, where the blast effect from a shell exploding within the confines of a formation would force it to break up, thus weakening defensive firepower and rendering individual bombers more vulnerable to attack.

The WGr. 21 rifled mortar launching tube took the form of an open cylinder constructed of rolled steel sheet 85 mm thick, butt-welded down its length. The external diameter was 250 mm and the length 1.3 m. One tube was suspended from beneath each underside wing surface of an Fw 190A-4/R6 by means of four bracing lugs and a central hook with a suspension bracket. Three retaining springs, located near the rear end of the tube, held the 112 kg shell with its 40 kg warhead in place, and a screw bolt, also at the rear end of the tube, prevented the shell from sliding out. In an emergency, the launching tube could be jettisoned by activating an electrically-primed explosive charge which severed the central hook.

The mortars were controlled from a cockpit panel containing two armament switches and a Revi 16B reflector gunsight. Two spin-stabilised shells were fired simultaneously when the pilot depressed a button on his control column.

The weapon was used in quantity for the first time against an American raid on 28 July 1943. Results were acceptable in as much as fragmentation from blasts did break up the bombers, and a number were claimed destroyed as an indirect result. Mortars were subsequently fitted to Bf 109s, Fw 190s, Bf 110s and Me 410s of several *Gruppen* operating in the Mediterranean and in the defence of the Reich.

Further trials continued through until mid-1944 with the aim of improving the WGr. 21. However, it was found that the lack of velocity (a maximum of 320 m per second) made the weapon extremely difficult to aim, and shells usually exploded harmlessly either short of the target or past it. The launch tubes also robbed German fighters, particularly the heavier *Zerstörer*, of their performance, and made them vulnerable to Allied fighters. Senior Luftwaffe fighter commanders did recognise the psychological effect of the mortars on bomber crews, but equally that when fitted to the Fw 190, for example, there was a loss in speed of 40–50 km/h, as well as a loss of ceiling and manoeuvrability. Furthermore, the lack of a range-measuring device resulted in an inability to control the point of detonation.

The Luftwaffe persisted in the use of WGr. 21 air-to-air mortars through to the closing weeks of the war. When the air-to-air bombing efforts of *Kdo. Stamp* using Me 262s proved fruitless, the OKL disbanded the unit and it was integrated into the *Stabsstaffel* of JG 7, where its Me 262A-1as were used to test deployment of mortars and R4M rockets. Two of the unit's aircraft are seen here at either Brandenburg-Briest or Parchim in the spring of 1945 undergoing fitment of launch tubes for 21 cm mortars (*EN Archive*)

As a makeshift measure, two of these weapons were mounted on bomb racks beneath the fuselages of a small number of Me 262s and tested operationally by the *Stabsstaffel* of JG 7, but to what effect is not known.

R4M ORKAN AIR-TO-AIR ROCKET

The fitment of 55 mm air-to-air rockets to the Me 262 created a potent combination of speed and destructive capability which heralded the dawn of a new age of airpower.

The *Rakete 4 kg Minenkopf* (R4M) rocket was manufactured by a consortium led by the Deutsches Waffen und Munitions Fabrik in response to the need for a form of armament that could be fired by a formation of fighters against enemy bomber formations singly or in salvos from extended range. It was hoped that such a weapon could create 'a dense fire-chain' that would be impossible for the bombers to avoid.

The R4M was an unrotated, rail- or tube-launched, single venturi, solid fuel-propelled, multi-fin stabilised missile, with the warhead contained in an exceptionally thin 1 mm sheet steel case enclosed in two pressed steel sections welded together and holding the Hexogen high-explosive charge. The missile bore a high charge weight-to-case weight ratio. The fuse was designed to discriminate between thin skin and main aircraft structure, and to penetrate 60–100 cm into a target aircraft before detonation to give maximum blast effect.

It was intended to launch the R4M from wooden under-wing racks positioned outside of the Me 262's engines, with the connections between the launch rack and the wing surface faired in to counteract the possibility of air eddies as much as possible. The standard launch rack, the EG.-R4M, measured approximately 700 mm in length, and each rocket was fitted with sliding lugs so that it could hang freely from the rack's guide rails. Each rocket was pushed from the rear of the rack along the guide rail until the rear sliding lug was arrested by a notch in the rail.

Firing trials took place at the end of October 1944 on a range at Strehla, and in March 1945 the first consignment of R4Ms was delivered to II./JG 7 at Parchim. It is believed they made their operational debut on

Twelve 55 mm R4M rockets have been loaded onto the wooden EG.-R4M launch rack fitted to the underside of the starboard wing of an Me 262A-1a from 9./JG 7. Another such rack would have been fitted to the underside of the port wing. Weighing 20 kg, more than a single rack could be carried under one wing, but as far as is known, this never happened. Visible is the running fox emblem of the *Geschwader* (*Author Collection*)

18 March against a USAAF raid on Berlin. Some 144 rockets were fired into the American formation from distances of between 400–600 m. Their effect was dramatic, with pilots reporting astonishing amounts of debris and aluminium fragments – pieces of wing, engines and cockpits flew through the air from aircraft hit by the rockets.

One pilot of III./JG 7, Oberfähnrich Walter Windisch, recalled, 'I experienced something beyond my conception. The destructive effect against the targets was immense. It almost gave me a feeling of being invincible'.

MAUSER MK 214 CANNON

The Me 262A-1a/U4, of which two were completed, was a standard aircraft fitted with a long-barrelled 50 mm Mauser MK 214 cannon in the nose space normally reserved for the four MK 108s. The origins of such a dubious configuration are believed to lie with Hitler, who, in January 1945, envisaged a weapon able to bring down bombers from outside their defensive fire-cones.

Projecting some two metres from the nose of the Me 262 and loaded with a 1.8 kg Mine projectile carrying about 450 g of high explosive, the cannon would have a muzzle velocity of approximately 900 m per second. The total weight of the shell was seven kilogrammes, and recoil was about 4000 kg. The total build weight, including ammunition, was 1000 kg. In the Me 262, installation of the MK 214 necessitated a redesign of the nosewheel gear so that it swivelled during retraction to lie flat in the nose.

During the afternoon of 25 April, Generalleutnant Adolf Galland's JV 44 (see Chapter 9) prepared 13 Me 262s in two formations, with one to carry out free-ranging patrols and the other to take on B-26 Marauders of the Ninth Air Force heading to Erding airfield and a neighbouring ammunition dump. In the latter group of Me 262s was the A-1a/U4.

Just before 1750 hrs, a single jet was spotted by B-26 crews of the 323rd Bombardment Group (BG) shadowing their formation way out to the right just after they had turned away from the target. This was probably the Me 262A-1a/U4. The jet initially circled around the Marauders to position itself for an attack from behind, closing in to about 500 yards, but without opening fire, before diving away to the right. It seems the 50 mm cannon in the A-1a/U4 had jammed or failed in some way – just as it had done in earlier attempts that month. This was the last known occasion that the Me 262 with an MK 214 was used in combat.

With a single MK 214 being built of around 390 individual parts, in reality the weapon was too complex and costly to be installed in any practical sense in an aircraft. Hitler's intentions came to naught.

The Me 262A-1a/U4 fitted with a Mauser 50 mm MK 214 cannon in its nose. Hitler placed considerable, but misguided, faith in the weapon. Messerschmitt test pilot Karl Baur is seen in the centre of the three men gathered at the aircraft's port side at Lechfeld. Baur flew the jet on 19 occasions before nightfighter ace Major Willi Herget took over tests for operational assessment. The aircraft was subsequently used by Generalleutnant Adolf Galland's JV 44. A second Me 262 was fitted with the weapon for trials (*EN Archive*)

CHAPTER EIGHT

NIGHT DEFENDER

Just as every type of Luftwaffe combat aircraft was capable of carrying bombs, so many of them too were able to operate as nightfighters. In the case of the British Mosquito, against which it was hoped that the Me 262 would prove a nemesis, the de Havilland aeroplane successfully fulfilled the day fighter, anti-shipping, reconnaissance, day/night bomber and nightfighter roles. By late 1944, despite the presence of Mosquitos flying with relative impunity over the Reich as nocturnal bombers and pathfinders, the night skies remained clear of Me 262 nightfighters to intercept them. In December 1944 that changed.

In a sense, what became the operational Me 262 nightfighter had its origins in the two-seat, dual-control trainer or *Schulflugzeug* version of the aircraft. In this variant, proposed during the summer of 1943, the fuselage was lengthened to accommodate an instructor in a seat behind the pupil pilot. The extended canopy was to feature side blisters to aid forward vision for the instructor, and although the capacity of the 900-litre rear fuel tank was necessarily and significantly reduced to 400 litres, this was to be compensated by two 300-litre drop tanks mounted on racks beneath the forward fuselage.

In early March 1944 this design was used as the basis for the Me 262B-1a, a two-seat trainer converted from a standard A-1a airframe, with conversion work to be carried out by Blohm und Voss at its facility at Wenzendorf, in northern Germany. The Me 262 S5 prototype – which flew for the first time on 28 April 1944 – was similar to the original *Schulflugzeug* in concept, although the fuel tanks were redesigned. From November 1944, the Deutsche Lufthansa workshops at Berlin-Staaken joined Blohm und Voss in the conversion process.

However, it was not until 1 September 1944, following a development meeting, that Messerschmitt issued an official overview for the development of a two-seat Me 262 nightfighter based on the Me 262B-1a trainer, but without dual controls. The second, rear seat was intended initially to accommodate a radar operator and house an array of radar, radio, Identification Friend or Foe (IFF) and guidance equipment, including FuG 25a *Erstling* IFF, FuG 16ZY VHF transceiver, FuG 101 radio altimeter and FuG 353 Zd *Rotterdam* Air Intercept radar. It was planned to enhance this in a second stage of development, which would see a FuG 218 *Neptun* set installed instead of the FuG 353, but with the former's SN 2 antennae replaced by a single *Morgenstern* antenna, and a FuG 120 for navigation. In this form the aircraft was planned as the Me 262B-2.

In November 1944, Leutnant Kurt Welter of 4./NJG 11 was assigned to the *Erprobungsstelle* at Rechlin in order to operationally test the Me 262A as a nightfighter. Precisely what qualified Welter to test-fly the Me 262 at this time is not clear, having previously flown operationally with 10./JG 300 – a Bf 109-equipped *Staffel* whose primary task was to hunt Mosquito bombers at night. Before that, he had enjoyed a noteworthy and somewhat remarkable operational record since September 1943, firstly with II./JG 300, then 5./JG 301, 5./JG 302 and 5. and 10./JG 300. Up to 28 October 1944, Welter had lodged 35 claims against enemy aircraft, all of which, bar five, were at night. He was decorated with the Knight's Cross on 18 October.

At least four Me 262A-1as – all already heavily-tested airframes – received additional equipment at Rechlin to enable night-flying, and Welter flew at least one of them on several occasions. From his brief experience, it seems Welter favoured the Me 262's deployment as a nightfighter, and in the first half of December moves were made towards the establishment of a dedicated Me 262 nightfighter unit under his command, with impetus coming from no less a figure than Göring.

On 11 December, the day Göring decreed the formation of a nightfighter test command, orders were also issued assigning the unit five two-seat Me 262B-1a/U1s, as the interim nightfighter variant was now classified, fitted with FuG 218. Welter had also received a small complement of pilots for what would become known as *Kommando Welter*. The unit was briefed to hunt and destroy Mosquitos, primarily using the same tactical principles of the single-seat, piston-engined *Wilde Sau* nightfighters whereby enemy aircraft were hunted freely and visually, usually over a target area, in cooperation with searchlight crews.

Leutnant Kurt Welter grins whilst leaning over the rear fuselage of what appears to be an Fw 190 fitted with the rod aerials for a FuG 217 AI set. After a brief period at the Rechlin test centre in late 1944, during which he assessed the Me 262 as a nightfighter, Welter was appointed leader of a *Kommando* named after him with the task of using the jet interceptor to combat RAF Mosquito night-bombers over the Berlin area. He was awarded the Oakleaves to the Knight's Cross in March 1945, and for many years was viewed as the Luftwaffe's highest-scoring jet pilot. However, recent research has questioned some of his 63 credited victories (*EN Archive*)

Post-war sources suggest that Welter flew his first missions as early as mid-December, and that he accounted for the downing of a Mosquito and a Lancaster on the nights of 11–12 and 12–13 December, respectively, but firm proof of these claims is lacking.

Before the year was out, *Kommando Welter* was boosted by the arrival at Rechlin of Feldwebel Karl-Heinz Becker, an instructor pilot already known to Welter from their time together at *Flugzeugführerschule* A/B 121 at Straubing – Welter had served as an instructor with this unit in 1942–43. Having recently converted onto the Fw 190, and anticipating orders sending him to JG 26, Becker was 'intercepted' from his new posting by Welter and was soon flying from Rechlin in an Me 262B-1a trainer, although any form of 'training' on the jet was, at best, hurried and rudimentary.

In the meantime, Welter was active throughout January and February 1945 and put in claims for another 18 enemy aircraft shot down during those months, of which, impressively, 13 were Mosquitos. But again, what would be accepted as conclusive proof of these claims is lacking.

For a brief period from 9 January 1945, *Kommando Welter* became tactically subordinate to II./NJG 11 based at Jüterbog-Waldlager. Around the middle of the month the unit relocated from Rechlin to Burg, near Magdeburg. Then, on 25 January, *Kommando Welter* was officially redesignated 10./NJG 11 with an establishment – in theory – of 12 Me 262s.

Four days earlier, the *Kommando* had suffered its first combat loss when Oberleutnant Heinz Bruckmann was killed following what may have been a daylight mission in which he pursued a USAAF reconnaissance Mosquito over northern Germany. His Me 262A-1a crashed into the Wittstocker Heide 15 minutes after take-off from Lärz when the aircraft refused to climb due to the trim control lever jamming in the nose-heavy position.

Ever on the move, Fritz Wendel reported to his superiors on what he found at Burg;

'A few days ago, *Nachtjagd-Kommando Welter*, attached to NJG 11, transferred to Burg, near Magdeburg. Oberleutnant Welter flies the Me 262 in nightfighter missions using the *"Wilde Sau"* method. Compared with the standard aircraft, some machines have ultra-violet lights and map illumination, but with an emergency turn-and-bank indicator only. Welter, who is the only pilot to have flown operationally at night with the aircraft, has already shot down three aircraft. A further five pilots are undergoing conversion training. The *Kommando* has six aircraft, all of which should be operational within a few days.'

To comply with a request from Professor Kurt Tank in his capacity as Chairman of the *Entwicklungssonderkommission Nacht- und Schlechtwetterjagd* (ESK-*Nachtjagd* – Special Commission for the Development of Night and Bad Weather Fighters), Messerschmitt issued a project description of the Me 262B-2 nightfighter on 18 January 1945.

British technical intelligence personnel walk past Me 262B-1a 'Red 12' of 10./NJG 11 at Schleswig-Jagel. The aircraft is fitted with FuG 218 antennae and twin Schloss 503 carriers under the forward fuselage to which have been fitted 300-litre drop tanks. The aircraft was eventually ferried to Britain (*EN Archive*)

The specification, intended to fully replace the interim work being carried out on the training aircraft by Deutsche Lufthansa at Berlin-Staaken, featured an extended central fuselage section to accommodate the second crewmember/navigator, increasing the aircraft's length from 10.6 m to 11.7 m, which, in turn, allowed additional fuel tankage of around 500 litres. This gave the nightfighter an endurance of two-and-a-quarter hours at 6000 m, which could be increased by 30 minutes if the aircraft was fitted with a pair of 300-litre drop tanks. Armament remained as per the A-1a, although allowance was made to increase this, if required, by incorporating a further two MK 108s or a pair of the new 'Sondergeräte' SG series of multi-barrelled 'shotgun blast' weapons then under development.

Six days later, on 24 January, the ESK was advised that one example of a single-seat Me 262 nightfighter fitted with FuG 218 had been completed and was destined for use by Oberleutnant Welter, who would test it operationally. The interim aircraft being prepared by DLH at Berlin-Staaken was expected in early February, and the prototype for the planned Me 262B-2 production model was due from Messerschmitt in March. The Commission expected the schedule for the B-2 to be maintained as a matter of priority, although the company was still unable to confirm when delivery of the remaining 15 such aircraft would be made.

However, despite this, neither the B-2, nor other designs submitted by Arado, Blohm und Voss, Dornier or Junkers, served to satisfy the ESK. On 27 January a new specification requirement was issued that called for a crew of three – pilot, navigator and radio operator – to man the aircraft, which would need to be entirely jet-propelled and be able to fly to a maximum speed of 900 km/h. The jet was to pack a punch, with its armament comprising the standard four nose-mounted MK 108s or new 30 mm MG 213 cannon. Two further such weapons were to be fitted in an obliquely-mounted arrangement to fire upwards at an angle of 70 degrees, while a pair of remotely-controlled MG 151s would serve as defensive guns.

Meanwhile, in terms of 'reality', by late January Messerschmitt was still unable to say when or where the 14 or 15 B-2 nightfighters would be built.

February did not begin well for the new 10./NJG 11, with the loss of two more pilots. On the 2nd, Oberleutnant Walter Eppelsheim was killed when his A-1a crashed north of Belzig while on a radio calibration and training flight, and two days later, Oberfeldwebel Paul Prandl met his fate when the A-1a he had just taken delivery of crashed near Brandenburg-Briest during its ferry flight to Burg. On the 5th, Welter crashed his aircraft west of Burg airfield. Feldwebel Becker was of the opinion that Welter had applied too much power, causing the engines to overheat. The Me 262 was damaged extensively.

At 1452 hrs on 15 February, Becker was ordered into the air in daylight to hunt for enemy reconnaissance aircraft in the Magdeburg area. This was his first operational mission, and he later reported;

'I climbed over the field to 7500 m altitude and from there I was guided to the enemy by Y-*Führung*. At 1554 hrs I made contact with an enemy Lightning. I saw the aircraft coming towards me, below and to the left, from the opposite direction. I immediately turned around and placed myself in a firing position from his rear, aiming downwards. I closed in on the target at high speed (around 900 km/h). The first burst of fire hit from 80 m away. The enemy aircraft exploded in the air in a huge burst of flames. I had to fly my machine through the explosion, and parts of it that came away damaged my left engine, so I had to make an emergency landing.'

The fighter control officer initially directed Becker to land at Paderborn, but then suggested Münster-Handorf. Unfortunately, he was unable to locate the latter, and running out of fuel, he was forced to come down in a field 1.5 km from Burg. Although his Me 262A-1a had sustained 20 per cent damage, Becker was credited with the destruction of an American F-5E Lightning of the 7th PRG at an altitude of 6200 m for his first victory, and the eighth claim of the *Staffel*.

In the first three weeks of March, 10./NJG 11 mounted sporadic, mostly nocturnal attacks against raids by RAF Bomber Command Mosquitos mainly around the Berlin area. Trying to catch the fast, all-wood bombers, however, was a tricky affair, and often resulted in frustration for the jet pilots, as Feldwebel Becker recalled;

'My thoughts were still preoccupied with the sortie I had flown over Berlin the previous night. At an altitude of 8500 m, I had a Mosquito illuminated by searchlights and in a good position to be attacked. However, as I manoeuvred my fighter into the correct angle to make a good shot, the rapid closing speed forced me to break off the first attack. With a top speed of 850 km/h, I was much faster than the Mosquito in front of me. I contacted my fighter controller to keep the Mosquito illuminated. I tried making a full turn to keep the enemy aircraft at the right range for a second attack.

'Beneath me an inferno was raging. Many areas of Berlin were on fire, and I observed many bomb explosions below. The sky was illuminated as it if it was daylight. I recognised my target in the searchlight beam as a tiny point. Only three beams were directed at the target at an obtuse angle. The aircraft was obviously heading for home at top speed. I closed the distance rapidly and could see the Mosquito clearly. I corrected my attack position, but the distance for opening fire was still too great. A final look at the turn indicator showed the arrow stood at the central position, and no yaw was encountered – I had experienced this last time, when my burst of fire missed.

'The sky was darker again, with very few stars providing any light. The searchlights slowly went out one-by-one, but there was still just enough light. The Mosquito was now in the crosshairs of my Revi and I dimmed the gunsight's light a little. Automatically, my hand gripped the control column more tightly. I barely noticed the sound of the engines. Suddenly, the last searchlights went out. Frantically, my eyes searched for the shadow of the Mosquito.

'I maintained direction. A few cirrus clouds. There was nothing to see other than a milky soup. I noticed ice crystals forming. All of a sudden I was out of the clouds. There were only stars – nothing else. Suddenly, the silhouette of the Mosquito appeared. I could see the shark fin of its tail clearly. I could see the blue-yellow exhaust flames from both engines – but it was too late. I was barely able to avoid the tail. There was no chance of firing. Too close. It would have been almost suicide to fly into the resulting explosion at that range. Part of me wanted to ram my opponent because all of my cannon had frozen. But such a thing was strictly forbidden by the fighter controller. I could not have bailed out safely at that speed. Bailing out at 850 km/h at 8000–9000 m without an ejection seat gave the pilot no chance.

'I could not reduce my speed. I can still see him clearly. I tried again from the right, with no change in position. Then there were more white, milky cirrus clouds. The Mosquito was gone. I must have overshot him. The chance had gone. I could have hit him with a stone, but despite all the technical assistance I was unable to shoot him down.

'I reversed course. Berlin was covered by red, fiery clouds. There was no more searchlight activity. The enemy was going home. Total frustration welled up inside me. But reality quickly returned. How much fuel did I have left? I returned to base. Gradually, I reduced altitude to 4000 m. Visibility was good. I could see light ground haze, which must have been the low ground near the Havel River. Everything else was in darkness. No lights. All of a sudden, the positioning searchlight at Burg airfield switched on. My compass heading was good.

'I took a left turn for my final approach. Speed was 400 km/h. Landing gear was down. There was a loud, rumbling noise from the wheel wells. The nose wanted to go up. The stick pressure was very strong. I lined up the aircraft in the direction of the runway. Airspeed was 260 km/h. Flaps were at 20 degrees. The landing lights were coming closer. At 240 km/h, the automatic slats extended. I increased flap position. Final approach was at 220–200 km/h.

'As I aimed for touchdown, I trimmed a little. I ignored the landing searchlight and approached the small landing lamps, reducing the risk of being seen by low-level nightfighters. The nose rose slightly, and pressure on the control column reduced this and I touched down softly at the beginning of the runway. I keep pressure on the rudder to keep the nose up as long as possible to reduce my landing speed. The nosewheel touched the runway and I intermittently applied the brakes. Disarming the four cannon, the end of the runway approached and I turned left. I shut off the engines, opened the canopy and pulled off my oxygen mask. I was happy to breathe fresh air again. My crew chiefs arrived to pick me up in the *Kettenkrad*. I reach into the right-hand pocket of my leather jacket and searched for a few real coffee beans – a luxury for nightfighter pilots. I crushed the bitter stuff between my teeth.'

On the night of 21–22 March, a force of 142 Mosquitos attacked the German capital in two waves, with some crews flying on both missions. The sky over the city was illuminated by the beams of

Oberleutnant Kurt Welter leans into the cockpit of Me 262B-1a 'Red 10' at Schleswig-Jagel to explain the instrument layout to the renowned Royal Navy test pilot Lt Cdr Eric Brown, attached to the Aerodynamics Flight of the Experimental Flying Detachment at RAE Farnborough. Next to Welter is Leutnant Jorg Czypionka of 10./NJG 11 (*EN Archive*)

some 60 searchlights, but the Flak was quiet so as to allow operations by nightfighters. At just after 2100 hrs, two Me 262s of 10./NJG 11, one flown by Becker, the other most probably by Welter, took off from Burg to intercept the first wave as it approached the southern edges of Berlin. He later reported;

'Over the target, I was badly hindered by problems with the engines. At 2132 hrs I got into a good firing position and fired at the enemy from 250 190 m from the right rear and below. I could see some hits in the fuselage and wings, which immediately caused fire to break out. I then moved away over the target. Due to parts breaking off the enemy aircraft, my left engine was damaged, which prevented me from further observation.'

Becker returned to Burg at 2154 hrs, and his claim – his second – was witnessed by Welter. For his part, Welter went on to claim two more Mosquitos, but there are no RAF losses to account for them.

Becker would prove his abilities two nights later when three jets from 10./NJG 11 led by Welter were sent up once more just before 2330 hrs to attack a force of 65 Mosquitos striking Berlin. Twenty minutes later, Becker spotted one of the raiders and opened fire with his four MK 108s 'right into the enemy'. The Mosquito exploded in front of him. Becker pulled up as debris flew over his left wing, and as he banked to the left he observed other parts falling to the ground, where they began to burn.

Moments later, Becker picked out another target. Turning to position himself behind, below and to the right of the enemy aircraft, he opened fire at a range of 150 m and saw hits strike the starboard wing near the engine. The Mosquito veered over to port, with smoke and flames streaming from beneath it. Becker watched the Mosquito spiral five times before it crashed into the ground. These were to be his third and fourth victories.

When the Mosquitos returned the following night (24–25 March), 10./NJG 11 again sent three Me 262s aloft into the searchlight zone. The night was clear and illuminated, and Becker quickly picked out one of the fast bombers. Attacking from behind, he saw his cannon shells strike the fuselage and wings of the enemy aircraft, but he was unable to observe it crash.

Moments later, a second Mosquito approached from ahead and above. Becker nosed down and turned towards the enemy machine, which began to slip away from the searchlight cones. Nevertheless, he was able to follow its contrails, and at 2132 hrs an at altitude of 9500 m, he opened fire from behind. On his first burst, several pieces broke away from the enemy aircraft. Becker banked to port, and a short while later saw burning wreckage on the ground south of Fehrbellin. This was the fifth Mosquito assumed to fall to his guns, despatched, so Becker thought, with just 15 30 mm mine shells.

'Under new ownership.' British servicemen pose for a snapshot atop Me 262B-1a/U1 'Red 12', to which have been applied RAF roundels in readiness for its flight to England. This aircraft was probably one of the last to be delivered to 10./NJG 11, arriving in mid-April 1945, and it replaced a previous 'Red 12' that had been lost on operations on the night of 27–28 March while being flown by Leutnant Herbert Altner (*EN Archive*)

While there were no Mosquito losses that night, one was badly damaged. A single 30 mm shell from Becker's MK 108s shattered its rudder and much of the horizontal stabilisers, but its pilot was able to return the aircraft to base.

On the evening of 27 March, RAF Bomber Command despatched another raid of 82 Mosquitos to Berlin. That night, 10./NJG 11 deployed the largest number of Me 262s to date – six in all. This operation was also notable for the fact that it saw the fateful debut of the *Staffel's* first two-seat, radar-equipped Me 262B-1a/U1 flown by Leutnant Herbert Altner, with Unteroffizier Reinhard Lommatzsch in the rear seat, both men having been posted in from 8./NJG 5.

According to Altner, he had collected the aircraft the day before from DLH at Berlin-Staaken after it, along with others, had been delivered there for conversion from Lechfeld. But on its first and only sortie over Berlin, Altner reduced his airspeed excessively, causing the jets to flame out. Restarting the engines in flight at night was not an option, and so the two airmen agreed to bail out. According to Altner, the bail-out technique from an Me 262 was as follows;

'1 Put aircraft in a nose-up attitude. Aircraft usually went into a dive after engine flame-out and fell like a stone.

2. Jettison canopy.

3. Release seat straps, stand on seat pan and from crouch position spring out of cockpit to gain sufficient tail clearance.'

Unfortunately, Lommatzsch was not adequately informed of this technique and he struck the tail as he exited. Having failed to deploy his parachute, he fell to his death. The Me 262 was lost.

Meanwhile, the remaining jets – all A-models – went into action. Becker later reported;

'At 2058 hrs I took off for a night operation over Berlin. Light conditions were poor, so I was not able to locate any targets in the searchlights. After I had to abandon one contact under such conditions, I flew back over the main area. I then spotted a Mosquito on an opposing course above me

The mottled nose of Me 262B-1a/U1 Wk-Nr 110305 'Red 8', with FuG 218 antennae, photographed while under evaluation in England (*EN Archive*)

with marked contrails, which I had previously observed dropping its bombs. I turned in from below and approached slowly. At 2138 hrs at an altitude of 8500 m, I saw the target clearly, and fired at a range of 150 m while climbing. I hit the target full on, and going into the left turn I saw some individual parts go down burning, hit the ground and scatter.'

At the end of March, the *Staffel* is recorded as having received 14 Me 262A-1s and three Me 262B-1a/U1s, although not all of these were still on strength by that time.

10./NJG 11's battle against the bombers continued throughout April, but the odds were against the

Luftwaffe groundcrew wait uncertainly near Me 262B-1a/U1, Wk-Nr 110305 'Red 8' at Schleswig-Jagel immediately post-war. The aircraft is still fitted with twin 300-litre drop tanks (*EN Archive*)

small jet unit. On the night of 2–3 April, Oberfeldwebel Heinrich von Stade, formerly a pilot with 10./JG 300, is believed to have collided with a Mosquito and both aircraft were lost. The unit was by then down to just four A-1s and two B-1a/U1s.

During daylight on the 3rd, five nightfighter jets engaged Mosquitos in the Berlin area and shot one down, and on the night that followed another Mosquito was subjected to a determined attack by an Me 262 that made four passes but was unable to prevent the damaged enemy bomber from escaping. After a few more missions, on 10 April, the *Staffel's* base at Burg was bombed by the Eighth Air Force. Four of the unit's nine jets were destroyed, and with operating conditions prohibitive at Burg, the decision was taken to relocate north to Lübeck-Blankensee.

The last known combat operation flown by 10./NJG 11 was on the night of 19–20 April, when two Me 262s purportedly claimed the destruction of two Mosquitos. The RAF then eased up its attacks on Berlin, sending a final wave of Mosquitos to the city on 20–21 April, by which time the Red Army was closing in on the capital from the east.

On 25 April, two of 10./NJG 11's Me 262A-1s, flown by Feldwebel Becker and his wingman, Leutnant Jorg Czypionka, who had joined the *Staffel* from II./NJG 11 in March, operated from an autobahn strip near Reinfeld. The two jets are believed to have been detailed to search for, and engage, enemy fighters in the area between Reinfeld and the Elbe. They duly encountered a formation of six Tempest Vs, but Becker's cannon failed and Czypionka's aim was wide. The two pilots then decided to head for Lübeck-Blankensee, where they ran into some Spitfires over the airfield. Czypionka's aircraft was hit and, uncertain if his undercarriage was working, he decided to belly-land the Me 262.

Lübeck was captured by the British on 2 May, and 10./NJG 11 made one final relocation before war's end to the airfield at Schleswig-Jagel, from where, one-by-one, its jets were taken by the victorious Allies as 'war prizes' for technical and tactical evaluation.

Recent research assigns 36 traceable claims to the Me 262s of *Kommando Welter* and 10./NJG 11. There may be that number again, many of which were claimed by Welter, but they remain inconclusive.

CHAPTER NINE

DAYLIGHT OPERATIONS PHASE 2

As the Luftwaffe's handful of Me 262 nightfighters defended the skies around Berlin in March 1945, so another, much larger Me 262 unit was operating in the defence of the approaches to the capital by day. At the beginning of the month, JG 7's three *Gruppen* of jet interceptors had moved to bases around Berlin and northern Germany. So would begin two months of intense operations in which the *Geschwader* would enjoy considerable success, suffer significant losses and endure grinding attrition in missions against the heavy bombers of the Eighth Air Force and their fighter escorts. The Me 262 pilots were nearly always heavily outnumbered when combating the massed American bomber formations, but at least they had the advantage of speed and destructive weaponry.

Just three days into March, the *Geschwader Stab* and III./JG 7 were scrambled to engage more than 1000 bombers, with an escort of nearly 700 fighters, targeting oil, armaments and transport targets across northern and central Germany. Against this raid, the *Stab* and Major Rudolf Sinner's III. *Gruppe* based at Brandenburg-Briest, Oranienburg and Parchim were able to muster 29 Me 262s. It was a mission that typified the combat that would follow in the weeks ahead.

The photographic record suggests that JG 7 was not afraid to experiment with camouflage schemes on its jet fighters – a sensible endeavour given the increasing threat of Allied fighter-bombers operating at will over the unit's bases. Here, Me 262A-1a 'Green 3' of the *Geschwaderstab* prepares to move off across a concrete taxiway at Brandenburg-Briest in the early spring of 1945. The aircraft, finished in a relatively rare application of streaked horizontal lines, has been fitted with a pair of 21 cm WGr. 21 air-to-air mortar tubes beneath the fuselage aft of the nosewheel (*EN Archive*)

The jets attacked the B-17s of the 3rd AD in line astern from 6000–7000 m between Braunschweig and Magdeburg. Hauptmann Heinz Gutmann, a former bomber pilot with III./KG 53 and a Knight's Cross-holder now flying with 10./JG 7, *Kommando Nowotny* veteran Leutnant Karl Schnörrer of 11./JG 7 and Oberfeldwebel Helmut Lennartz of 9./JG 7 each claimed a Flying Fortress destroyed, while Oberfähnrich Heinz Russel of 9./JG 7 and Oberfeldwebel Büchner managed to shoot down a P-47 and P-51, respectively. Büchner, who also claimed a B-17, later recalled;

'We broke through the fighter escorts but then found ourselves under massive defensive fire from the bombers' turret gunners. When we were about 1000 m from the bombers, Gutmann's cockpit flashed with fire and his fighter sheared away from our formation and dived away vertically. I think he might have been killed outright, as he did not attempt to bail out.'

Gutmann's Me 262 hit the ground a few kilometres south of Braunschweig.

Russel, another former *Kommando Nowotny* pilot, targeted a B-17, but just as he opened fire with his MK 108s, a Thunderbolt flew across his path and it blew apart in mid air.

Over Magdeburg, Me 262s from 10. and 11./JG 7 took on more B-17s, as well as the 219 B-24s of the 2nd AD bombing the oil refinery at Rothensee. Oberfeldwebel Heinz Arnold shot down a B-17 and a P-47, while Major Sinner claimed a B-24. Initially, his *Schwarm* had made a frontal attack against the Liberators, but without success. So, despite the challenge of passing through the formation without collision, Sinner went in accompanied only by his wingman, Leutnant Fritz Müller, from the rear, but as he did so all four of his MK 108s jammed just after he had opened fire on a selected B-24. As he broke away, Sinner noticed a flash on the bomber's wing. The following day, the downing of a Liberator in the same location that Sinner's combat had taken place was reported by a local Flak unit, and he was belatedly credited with the victory.

Six *Viermots* and three escort fighters had fallen to the guns of JG 7. Although the USAAF claimed six jets shot down, such losses are not recorded on the German side.

Fifteen days later, on 18 March, JG 7 deployed the new R4M rocket for the first time against a force of nearly 1200 bombers attacking railway and armaments factories in the Berlin area. They were escorted by 426 fighters. The jets of 9. *Staffel* put up six aircraft, with each jet carrying two underwing batteries of 12 rockets. Oberfähnrich Walter Windisch, who had two victories to his credit by the time he joined JG 7 from JG 52, recalled;

'The launching grids for the rockets were not of optimum design – they were still too rough and ready. Compared with conventionally powered aircraft, when you went into a turn with the Me 262, flying became a lot more difficult because the trimming was not too good.'

Nevertheless, after firing their rockets, the pilots of JG 7 were astonished at their effect on the bombers. In the R4M they had a weapon which they could use at a range much greater than their 30 mm cannon. One pilot recalled observing a B-17 'crumple in the air' as its wing took a direct hit from a rocket.

Very different weaponry was being used by the Me 262 bombers of KG 51 on what was still optimistically referred to as the Western Front. Here, German ground forces were being pushed back ever eastwards. The Americans took München-Gladbach on 1 March and at last reached the Rhine at Neuss opposite Düsseldorf on the 3rd. While on a tour of the Western Front, Prime Minister Winston Churchill visited the town of Jülich, thus standing on German soil.

Despite this Allied wave, KG 51 doggedly fought back. Throughout the first half of March, the *Stab*, I. and II. *Gruppen* mounted regular, low-level sorties against American troop concentrations and clusters of armour, and occasionally Allied-occupied airfields. The favoured tactics were, if possible, to strike at dawn or dusk and, depending on the type of target, the favoured ordnance was either 250 kg bombs or AB 250 bomb containers loaded with 17 SD 10A *Splitterbomben.*

For example, on the morning of 2 March 26 Me 262s from II./KG 51 at Mühlheim took off to target tanks and troops of the US Ninth Army in the Düren area. Attacks were made through AA fire at Rheindahlen, Erkelenz, Wickrath, Bedburg and Elsdorf. Two jets broke off the action due to technical faults and the *Gruppe* reported the Me 262A-2a flown by Hauptmann Fritz Abel, *Staffelkapitän* of 5./KG 51, missing. He had been shot down in the Aachen/Nijmegen area.

That afternoon, Me 262s from II./KG 51 returned to the Düren area, with two jets targeting the town, one bombing Wickrath and another attacking Horrem from 4500 m down to 1500 m. Unteroffizier Golde of 6. *Staffel* dropped his SD 250s in horizontal flight over Heppendorf. Although no aircraft were lost to enemy action, two Me 262A-2as were forced to abandon the mission owing to technical problems. They made emergency landings at Mühlheim. Other clashes took place between KG 51 and USAAF P-47s, although neither side suffered any losses. One American pilot reported that 'it was like rhinos chasing gazelles'.

A key target for KG 51 became the bridge at Remagen. Typical was the mission of 13 March in which four Me 262s from II./KG 51 took off from Rheine and made an attack between 0905 and 1002 hrs at an altitude of 5000 m on river crossings in the bridgehead area. The jets were each equipped with two AB 250 containers filled with SD 10 anti-personnel bombs. Two aircraft were lost on the return flight to Rheine, one making an emergency landing near Lüdinghausen due to fuel shortage. The other pilot bailed out following an engine failure, his aircraft crashing at Neuenkirchen, southwest of Rheine.

Later in the day, 24 Me 262s from I. and II./KG 51 flew an attack on enemy concentrations and road traffic in the Kleve–Xanten–Emmerich area. Two aircraft broke off due to technical defects and jettisoned their 500 kg containers of ten kilogramme anti-personnel bombs. The eventual capture of the bridge at Remagen by the Americans rendered the airfields in the Rheine area untenable for the Luftwaffe and would force KG 51 to move, first to Giebelstadt and then to Leipheim, in Bavaria.

On the last day of the month, KG 51 reported 79 Me 262s on strength, and these aircraft were ordered to attack the bridges around Hanau and Allied troops in the Mannheim–Heidelburg area. Twelve aircraft from I./KG 51 took off from Leipheim to attack the bridges and enemy troops in

In a typical dusk scene at Rheine, a *Kettenkrad* pulls Me 262A-2a 9K+BK of 2./ KG 51 out of a camouflaged dispersal set amongst fir trees towards the runway. By the spring of 1945, all Luftwaffe units and their airfields operated under the constant risk of Allied bombing and strafing attacks (*EN Archive*)

the early morning. Three dropped two 250 kg bombs each, another an AB 250 with SD 10 bombs and a fifth jet dropped an AB 500 with the same SD 10 load on the pontoon bridge south of Hanau. Thick fog obscured the results of the attack. The Me 262A-2a of Leutnant Lange of 1./KG 51 was hit by AA fire during his glide-attack through fog at 1000 m over the target, but he released his SD 250s and returned safely.

Three more aircraft dropped two AB 250 containers and one AB 500 container on another temporary bridge west of Hanau, with hits on enemy troops on the bridge being observed. A further two jets from I./KG 51 dropped two 250 kg bombs on a transport column south of Hanau, but another machine was forced to break off its attack due to a technical fault. No losses were suffered.

Three Me 262s from I. *Gruppe* flew a further similar mission later that morning. One dropped a 250 kg bomb on the bridge west of Hanau and another made an attack on a stationary transport column west of the town. Again, no losses were sustained. II./KG 51 was also involved in similar operations.

In the afternoon, a third operation was mounted against enemy columns on the road from Amorbach to Walldürn. Over the target area, Leutnant Lange attacked a convoy of 16 light vehicles southeast of Rippberg-im-Odenwald with his Me 262A-2a in a gliding attack from 2000 m, releasing his ordnance at 1300 m. While in the target area, he was attacked by six P-47s, but he was able to out-manoeuvre them. He and another pilot returned safely to Leipheim. In the afternoon, aircraft from II./KG 51 also targeted American troops near Hardheim, northeast of Walldürn.

During March, 20 Me 262A-1a/U3 short-range reconnaissance aircraft were produced and delivered to NAGr. 1 and NAGr. 6. Attempts to convert 1./NAGr. 13 seem to have faltered, however, with 16. *Fliegerdivision* reporting that the *Staffel* was still without aircraft. Me 262 reconnaissance flights over the Western Front remained sporadic at best, although their value to German commanders was in no doubt.

Early in the month, jets of 2./NAGr. 6 made a visual reconnaissance of the Bischweiler–Zabern–Brumath area, while another photographed roads in the Wantzenau, Zabern and Erstein areas. An Me 262 of NAGr. 6 was assigned to carry out a photo-reconnaissance mission over the Nijmegen–Emmerich–Goch–Kleve area on the 19th, but the sortie was aborted owing to heavy ground mist. However, another such sortie was sent out over the western bank of the Rhine from Xanten, south of Düsseldorf. An indication of how important these reconnaissance operations were viewed by the German command can be seen by the fact that airfield cover for the missions was provided by no fewer than 27 Fw 190s of I. and IV./JG 26.

On 23 March, *Stab*/NAGr. 1 was reported as equipping with the Me 262 at Lechfeld and the *General der Aufklärer* issued orders that another reconnaissance *Staffel*, 1./NAGr. 13, should be assigned for conversion to the Me 262 also at Lechfeld. On the 25th, this *Staffel* was preparing to give up its Bf 109s at Oedheim for conversion to the jet. By the 27th, *Stab*/NAGr. 6 was at Vörden, 1./NAGr. 6 at Ahlhorn and 2./NAGr. 6 at Münster-Handorf, while on the 29th, *Stab*/NAGr. 1 with two aircraft and 1. *Staffel* with seven aircraft were at Fritzlar-Nord.

To the south of Würzburg, from Giebelstadt, the former bomber pilots of I./KG(J) 54 were thrown into action against American bombers amidst the

Oberfeldwebel Friedrich Gentsch of 7./KG(J) 54 looks out from the cockpit of Me 262A-1a B3+BC at Neuburg/Donau in March 1945. Just visible is a white nose tip and the aircraft's individual letter applied to the nosewheel door. There is also a yellow diagonal line running from the forward base of the canopy to the wing root at the trailing edge (*EN Archive*)

most disruptive of operating conditions. In the early afternoon of 1 March, as more than 1000 B-17s and B-24s struck at marshalling yards across central and southern Germany, eight Me 262s of Major Otfried Sehrt's *Gruppe* engaged the *Viermots* reported to be in the Nördlingen–Ingolstadt area. They made contact at 8000 m over Treuchtlingen, and a B-17 and one of the P-51 escorts were claimed shot down, although the USAAF reported the loss of two B-17s due to a mid-air collision. Leutnant Hans-Peter Häberle of 2./KG(J) 54 and Feldwebel Josef Herbeck of 1. *Staffel* were shot down by P-51s during the encounter.

Feldwebel Heinrich Griens of 3. *Staffel* was lost to fighters the next day shortly after taking off to intercept bombers attacking the synthetic fuel plants, while his *Staffelkamerad*, Feldwebel Günther Görlitz, was forced to bail out wounded.

Attrition gnawed at the *Geschwader*, not just as a result of air combat but also from regular USAAF bombing and strafing attacks on Giebelstadt that resulted in losses in aircraft, pilots and groundcrew. At 1015 hrs on the 21st, Me 262s from I./KG(J) 54, along with JG 7, were airborne and directed by 1. *Jagddivision* to intercept wide-ranging operations by the Eighth Air Force that included attacks on the jet bases. The *Gruppe* accounted for one B-17 shot down, but it lost Unteroffizier Willi Ehrecke of 1. *Staffel*, who was shot down but seen to bail out. However, he was posted missing and never returned.

The USAAF operations that day spelled disaster for III./KG(J) 54 under the command of Knight's Cross-holder Hauptmann Eduard Brogsitter. No fewer than 364 B-24s of the Fifteenth Air Force bombed its base at Neuburg/Donau and, according to subsequent *Luftgau* reports, in the process destroyed 12 Me 262s and damaged a further 38. The runways and taxiways were also heavily damaged, meaning flying operations became impossible.

Meanwhile, conditions were a little more sedate for Generalleutnant Adolf Galland's small and embryonic Me 262 unit, which was forming up at Brandenburg-Briest. Galland had elected to self-designate his unit *Jagdverband* (JV) 44, and he had been ordered by General Karl Koller, Chief of the Luftwaffe Operations Staff, to relocate to southern Germany in order to operate in the defence of the aircraft manufacturing plants and fuel and ammunition storage facilities in the region which were being targeted relentlessly. Galland selected the airport at Munich-Riem as the base for future operations.

However, although the dismissed *General der Jagdflieger* had managed to muster adequate numbers of ground personnel and equipment, he still lacked pilots and aircraft. As late as 31 March, just nine Me 262s had been delivered from the factories to JV 44, of which one was undergoing repair. Six more were unserviceable as a result of enemy air attacks on Brandenburg-Briest. Another two aircraft were expected to arrive from training units. By comparison, JG 7 reported 79 of its aircraft as serviceable that day.

At dawn on the 31st, with the arrival of clear weather and presumably with at least some aircraft available, Galland ordered half of his meagre cadre of 20 or so pilots to ferry the jets south to Riem under the leadership of Oberst Steinhoff. One-by-one the small formation comprising renowned aces such as Steinhoff and Hohagen, as well as a number of instructor pilots assigned to the unit, arrived at Riem without incident, along with a pair of twin-engined Si 204s carrying signals and other equipment. The unit would soon be in action.

Slowly, but surely, the Third Reich was being crushed from both the east and the west. In early April 1945, Adolf Hitler moved his headquarters to a bunker deep beneath his Chancellery in Berlin. On the Western Front, although Allied forces had completed their encirclement of the Ruhr, KG 51 continued to fly its bombing missions. The first day of the month saw 19 Me 262s from the unit make gliding attacks against enemy columns and positions with SD 250s and AB 250/SD 10s west of Würzburg–Bad Mergentheim. After dropping their bombs, some jets strafed at low-level, and the *Geschwader* made attacks on other targets during the day.

But there was pressure mounting from within the Luftwaffe, for with the need to strengthen the Me 262 fighter units, on 2 April I./KG 51 was ordered to transfer some of its aircraft to JG 7 – a sign that production was failing, losses were accruing and that air defence rather than offensive bombing was the priority.

By 8 April I./KG 51 was at Leipheim under Major Heinz Unrau with 15 Me 262s (11 serviceable) and II./KG 51 was at Linz and Hörsching under Hauptmann Hans-Joachim Grundmann with six jets (two serviceable). To 10 April, KG 51 had apparently received a total allocation of 242 Me 262s. Of these, 88 had been lost through enemy activity and an astonishing 146 to other reasons – presumably accidents, crashes or destruction due to bombing prior to delivery.

Leutnant Heinrich Haeffner of 2./KG 51 described the environment in which I. *Gruppe* found itself on the 10th;

'I have received a new Me 262. Our aircraft are hidden in the forest to the left and right of the Autobahn. American fighters are constantly over our airfield and Marauder units carpet the field with bombs. At 1106 hrs, I take off from the Autobahn for a mission to Crailsheim. The aircraft was pulled onto the Autobahn with a *Kettenkrad*. Then the turbines were started and we headed off on an easterly course. The landing took place from the west in order that we could quickly be hidden again in the forest. I was elated not to have become easy prey for enemy fighters on landing. At 1419 hrs, I took off with two 250 kg bombs towards Roth, near Nürnberg.

I attacked a bridge there. At 1716 hrs, another mission to Roth. There is a lot of anti-aircraft fire in the target area.'

As the battlefields in the West became increasingly fluid, more than ever reconnaissance was needed. With a very small number of jets and dwindling fuel availability, 1./NAGr. 6 at Lechfeld and 2./NAGr. 6 at Kaltenkirchen and Hohne did their best to maintain some kind of useful contribution by observing Allied movement along what remained of the Western Front.

With his canopy closed, the pilot of Me 262A-1a/U3 'White 2' of 1./NAGr. 1 waits for clearance to head for take-off on another reconnaissance mission from Zerbst at the beginning of April 1945. Clearly visible is the bulged fairing on the nose to allow fitment of an Rb 50/30 camera (*EN Archive*)

However, 1./NAGr. 1 was ordered to Zerbst with its few Me 262s in early April.

Oberfeldwebel Fritz Oldenstädt of 2./NAGr. 6 took off during the evening of 2 April on a reconnaissance of the Paderborn–Kassel area, but shortly after take-off flame was seen trailing from his Me 262's left engine. Oldenstädt made a rough forced-landing at Heeke, writing his aircraft off in the process. The next day, *Stab*/NAGr. 6 moved to Fassberg, and on the 5th 'the four available' Me 262s conducted reconnaissance flights over the Ruhr area and from Lüneberg Heath to Magdeburg.

By 6 April 1./NAGr. 1 was operational with seven Me 262s (three serviceable) at Zerbst. The unit was to cover the 'central area as far west as Frankfurt/Main'. A *Rotte*, consisting of one fighter and one reconnaissance aircraft, flew the unit's first sortie. It also 'borrowed' an Me 262B-1a trainer from III./EJG 2, one of seven such aircraft that the latter unit had 'handed over to operational units', leaving it with 'none left'. Prevailing operating conditions were illustrated by reports from Lechfeld on the 8th that eight pilots of 1./NAGr. 1 were training on the single borrowed Me 262.

The *Staffel* flew a reconnaissance operation of the Mülhausen–Langensalza–Gotha area, but sorties by three other aircraft were broken off due to technical problems. On 8 April, *Stab*/NAGr. 1 was ordered to join 1. *Staffel* at Zerbst, 2./NAGr. 1 was to go to Körnelitz and 3./NAGr. 1 to Altengrabow. Meanwhile, on the 9th, *Stab*/NAGr. 6 was at Lechfeld under Major Heinz Schultze – but without aircraft – along with 2./NAGr. 6 under Herward Braunegg with seven Me 262s, of which three were serviceable.

Plans to bring more bomber conversion units into operation had foundered by early April. On the 3rd, the OKL noted that the proposed re-equipping of KG(J) 27 with the Me 262 was not possible and recommended that the *Geschwader* be disbanded, with its pilots sent to bolster fighter and ground-attack units. By the end of the month, a similar fate befell the planned establishments of III./KG(J) 30 and I. and II./KG(J) 6.

Such rationalisation failed to prevent initiatives taking place which had been born of desperation. Such was the case on 7 April when the volunteer *Schulungslehrgang 'Elbe'*, known also as *Sonderkommando 'Elbe'*, carried out a mass strike using piston-engined fighters against a large Eighth Air Force raid attacking 16 airfield, military, industrial and rail targets across northern and central Germany. The intention was for '*Elbe*' to use conventional armament, but also to ram enemy *Viermots*, if necessary,

A scene of devastation at Zerbst, photographed shortly after the USAAF bombing raid on 10 April 1945. In the foreground are three Me 262s of I./KG(J) 54. The machine at left and the one in the centre, possibly Wk-Nr 111674, appear relatively unscathed, while the aircraft at right remains in its bare metal and filler paste factory finish, and is missing its canopy and tail fin leading edge where the tail meets the fuselage (*EN Archive*)

in order to bring them down. The indoctrinated young fighter pilots volunteered on the understanding that there was 'little possibility of returning'.

Shortly after 1230 hrs, 15 Me 262s from I./KG(J) 54 were airborne from Zerbst, along with another 54 from III./JG 7, in order to divert the American fighter escort. On his approach towards the bombers, the *Staffelkapitän* of 1./KG(J) 54, Hauptmann Werner Tronicke, shot down a Flying Fortress, and on a second pass he scored hits on another B-17, while at the same time being struck by defensive fire. Wounded, and with Mustangs on his tail, Tronicke banked his Me 262 away and attempted to reach Hagenow airfield. As his jet took more strikes from the P-51s, he was forced to bail out close to the airfield. However, Tronicke's success against the bombers was an isolated one. His place as commander of 1. *Staffel* would be taken by Oberleutnant Leopold Beck.

The jet airfields were being pulverised. On 9 April the Eighth Air Force bombed the bases in southern Germany, and on the 10th it was the turn of those located in the north. In response, all 21 of the Me 262s which were categorised as *'einsatzklar'* (operationally ready) of the 37 on strength with I./KG(J) 54 took off to engage. But no sooner were they heading for the bombers than 75 B-17s of the 3rd AD dropped 222 tons of bombs on Zerbst.

Meanwhile, in similar circumstances to those that befell Tronicke three days earlier, Leutnant Paul Pallenda of I./KG(J) 54 claimed a B-17 shot down in his first pass, but on his following approach his Me 262 was hit by return fire from a second target. He attempted to reach an alternative landing ground to the north, but crashed to his death near Genthin.

Leutnant Jürgen Rossow of 3./KG(J) 54 accounted for one B-17 destroyed and another damaged. After leaving the bombers, he headed for Stendal, but he was fired upon by P-51s and in the ensuing emergency landing Rossow was badly wounded.

Leutnant Gerhard Becker, also of 3. *Staffel*, claimed the destruction of a Flying Fortress, then found another flying alone, having, it seemed, already suffered combat damage. Becker administered the coup de grâce. However, unable to return to Zerbst, he tried to land at Barby, but as he did so he was bounced by Mustangs and had to bail out. While hanging from his parachute, it is believed he was again attacked by the Mustangs, but Becker survived to land in a field with his parachute shot through.

I./KG(J) 54 would fly only a few more sorties before the end of the war. By mid-April, at Munich-Riem, JV 44 was flying regular missions against the US tactical air forces attacking targets in southern Germany and Austria. The unit had relatively few aircraft, but paradoxically, Galland, like some Pied Piper, had been joined by a growing clique of highly experienced and highly decorated aces. Aside from Steinhoff and Hohagen, from the day fighter arm came Oberst Gunther Lützow (Knight's Cross with Swords, 108 victories), Major Gerhard Barkhorn (Knight's Cross with Swords, 301 victories), Hauptmann Walter Krupinski (Knight's Cross with Oak Leaves, 197 victories) and Major Hans Grünberg (Knight's Cross, 82 victories). Major Wilhelm Herget (Knight's Cross with Oak Leaves, 63 victories [57 at night]) came from nightfighters, and Major Heinrich Brücker (Knight's Cross, 250 missions) arrived from the *Schlachtflieger*.

In reality, however, much of the unit's combat flying was undertaken by experienced, but more junior officers and NCO instructors from the fighter schools. But conditions at Riem were no better than those at Zerbst. According to Galland, 'the rumour was that the American fighter-bombers would even attack a stray dog'.

On 10 April – the day the Eighth Air Force bombed the northern jet bases – three Me 262s of JV 44 were destroyed and another three damaged during a low-level attack on Riem by P-51s. Unteroffizier Johann-Karl Müller, who had flown Fw 190s in the ground-attack role with II./SG 10 on the Eastern Front, took off mid-morning to intercept a flight of P-47s, probably from the Ninth Air Force's 36th FG, over Augsburg. Müller shot a Thunderbolt down over the city and returned to Riem an hour later. However, by the end of the day, of 13 newly delivered Me 262s, JV 44 reported 11 as destroyed by enemy action, with another lost due to 'other causes'.

On the 16th, Galland led as many as 14 jets, some equipped with R4M rockets, to intercept B-26 Marauders. Galland claimed two of the bombers shot down, which corresponds to two lost by the 322nd BG that day.

To the north, JG 7 had absorbed the loss of several of its seasoned pilots. On 10 April Oberleutnant Franz Schall, commander of 10. *Staffel*, died when his Me 262 rolled into a bomb crater, turned over and exploded following an emergency landing at Parchim. Schall had been awarded the Knight's Cross on 10 October 1944, and had recorded his 133rd victory on the day of his death. A formidable fighter pilot, he had shot down 61 Il-2s over the Eastern Front. Also lost on the 10th was Oberleutnant Walter Wagner, *Staffelkapitän* of 3./JG 7. In addition to pilot and ground personnel casualties, JG 7 had suffered the loss of 27 Me 262s, with a further eight damaged.

But Weissenberger's men did not give up. On 17 April, 300 fighters from the Ninth Air Force attacked German airfields at Saatz, Pilsen and Prague-Rusin. About 20 Me 262s from JG 7 managed to take off, with Major Wolfgang Späte, who coordinated operations for I./JG 7, Oberleutnant Walter Bohatsch, recently

Oberst Johannes Steinhoff receives updates on the air situation by telephone link from JV 44's operations room while surrounded by the unit's pilots at Munich-Riem in April 1945. Indentifiable, from left to right are Hauptmann Walter Krupinski, Major Erich Hohagen, Oberst Günther Lützow (in the leather overcoat, reading), Steinhoff (seated), Fahnenjunker-Oberfeldwebel Klaus Neumann (leaning forward, wearing a forage cap), Oberleutnant Klaus Faber and Unteroffizier Eduard Schallmoser (partially obscured, also wearing a forage cap) (*Author Collection*)

appointed as *Staffelkapitän* of 1./JG 7, and Oberleutnant Fritz Stehle each claiming a bomber in the Dresden area. The Eighth Air Force reported three separate attacks by jets, all of which were foiled by the fighter escort. A B-17 was shot down near Berlin by Hauptmann Eder of III./JG 7, now back in action following his injuries sustained in February, while in the Prague area, III. *Gruppe* pilots Leutnant Fritz Müller, Oberfeldwebel Otto Pritzl and Oberfeldwebel Anton Schöppler all claimed kills.

During the early afternoon of the 18th, hundreds of aircraft from the USAAF's Eighth, Ninth and Fifteenth Air Force's attacked railway targets and fuel dumps across southern Germany and around the Prague–Pilsen areas. Overwhelmingly outnumbered, JV 44 sent up six Me 262s, at least half of them carrying R4Ms, to take on the bombers. The small formation was broken down into two three-aircraft *Ketten*, with Galland leading the first *Kette* accompanied by Oberleutnant Franz Stigler and Leutnant Klaus Neumann, while Steinhoff, Krupinski and Leutnant Gottfried Fährmann formed the second. The six jets were flown by what must have been one of the most illustrious groupings of Luftwaffe pilots ever assembled to fly one mission – one Generalleutnant, four holders of the Knight's Cross and five pilots accounting for almost 550 victories.

Galland was airborne first, with Stigler next and Neumann following. Behind came Steinhoff, followed by Krupinski to his left and Fährmann on the right. As the second *Kette* rolled along the strip reaching 200 km/h, Steinhoff's port wing suddenly dropped as his mainwheel struck some debris left on the field from the previous day's bombing attack. The Me 262 began to swerve to the left, dangerously close to Krupinski, who was still powering behind. He hauled his control column back and took off just in time to avoid a collision, flying right over Steinhoff's Me 262, which was now heading irreversibly – and still at speed – towards an embankment at the end of the strip. A second or so later, Krupinski became aware of an explosion which buffeted his aircraft. Neumann was also airborne, but realising something was very wrong, for an instant looked back, horrified, towards the ground. Steinhoff's aircraft was now an inferno.

Flying through the drifting smoke, the five remaining jets continued with the mission, but it proved a fruitless sortie. When the pilots returned they were certain Steinhoff had been killed. But he had escaped, saved by the self-contained metal cockpit sub-assembly which held the Me 262's instrument panel and electrical controls, control column and rudder, throttles, seat and battery, and which was intended to break free in the event of a crash. But although alive, Steinhoff had been very badly burned.

On 19 April, some 20 Me 262s from JG 7 and I./KG(J) 54 operated in scattered elements against bombers in the Dresden–Aussig–Pirna area. The jets claimed five B-17s, a figure which tallies with USAAF losses. Four of the bombers fell to one pass by JG 7 when six jets attacked B-17s of the 3rd AD as they made their bomb run just after midday when the escort was 'thin'. A fifth flying Fortress went down to a jet making a pass at 'eight o'clock' against the high squadron of the third group bombing Pirna, the attack being made between the target and the rally point. The successful German pilots included Späte, Schöppler, Bohatsch, Oberleutnant Hans Grünberg of I./JG 7 (about to go to JV 44) and Oberfeldwebel Hubert Göbel of III./JG 7.

The Me 262 reconnaissance units kept operating up to the end. On 1 May, Leutnant Tetzner of 2./NAGr. 6 made his last flight from Kaltenkirchen over Hannover–Magdeburg–Schwerin–Lübeck to land at Schleswig-Land (Jagel). Over Bad Oldesloe, he had spotted two British fighters 200 m away to the side of him, but chose not to engage them and flew off into the cover of cloud. On the 4th, on orders from his *Kommandeur*, Major Schultze, Oberfeldwebel Oldenstädt flew the last reconnaissance mission from Hohn, in Schleswig-Holstein, that evening. On the morning of the 5th, Schultze and Oldenstädt received orders to take a two-seat Me 262 to Norway, but the aircraft's engines were faulty so they were unable to execute the flight. In the late morning, British tanks reached the airfield, and the German airmen set about blowing up their aircraft.

A US serviceman peers into the cockpit of the wrecked airframe of Me 262A-1a/U3 'White 2' of 1./NAGr. 1 believed to be at Bernburg. The bulged nose camera fairing is visible (*EN Archive*)

Also on 4 May, in the south, Galland, now wounded following an encounter with a P-47 on 26 April, had arranged for some of JV 44's remaining jets to fly to Hötting airfield, on the outskirts of Innsbruck, where they would be relatively 'safe' from the Soviets, but abandoned. Early that same morning at the unit's new base at Salzburg-Maxglan, Hauptmann Krupinksi, accompanied by a mechanic, rode in a *Kettenkrad* tow tractor along the line of Me 262s that remained parked on the airfield and dropped a hand grenade into the engine intakes of each aircraft. One after another, the grenades exploded, rendering the Jumo 004 engines useless.

When the end did come, the Me 262 interceptor, bomber and reconnaissance *Gruppen* were scattered across Germany, Austria and around Prague, in Czechoslovakia. At dawn on 7 May, Oberleutnant Heinrich Haeffner of 2./KG 51 was at Prague-Ruzyne, from where he would fly his last ground-attack mission;

'At first light the groundcrew got my machine ready for take-off. As I climbed into my aircraft and the Riedel motor was started, there was the first sound of machine gun fire. However, I brought both turbines up to full power and I took off immediately. I attacked enemy troops south of the airfield with bombs, rockets and cannon.'

Haeffner was in the air for 45 minutes, landing at 0610 hrs. He took off on a second sortie over the airfield at 1025 hrs, but received light damage from ground fire to his aircraft as he got airborne. He flew over the enemy positions and fired rockets into their vehicles, before heading for Saaz. By the time he landed, his Me 262 had suffered so much damage that it was not repairable.

Encapsulating the situation in the north was the bald report issued by *Luftflotte Reich* on 7 May. 'II./JG 7 is reported at Gettorf minus aircraft'.

In what is believed to have been the final jet interceptor sortie of the war, the acting commander of I./JG 7, Oberleutnant Stehle, shot down a Yak-9 over Czechoslovakia on 8 May whilst flying one of the last airworthy aircraft of the composite battle command *Gefechtsverband Hogeback*. Stehle then made his way to Fassberg to surrender.

APPENDICES

COLOUR PLATES COMMENTARY

1
Me 262 V5 Wk-Nr 262 000 0005 PC+UE, Augsburg, Germany, summer 1943
This aircraft, which was used extensively for testing, was finished in a base coat of RLM 76 (*graublau*), with wing and fuselage uppersurfaces in RLM 74 (*graugrün*)/75 (*grauviolett*). The mottling was applied heavily, with the tail assembly being predominantly RLM 74. The code was in black, the *Balkenkreuz* in white outline only and the prototype number on the tailfin also in white.

2
Me 262 S1 Wk-Nr 130006 VI+AF, Lechfeld, Germany, spring 1944
This aircraft was finished in an overall base coat of RLM 76, with wide areas of RLM 75 applied around the fuselage in the cockpit area, while the rear fuselage and tail areas were left mainly in RLM 76. A large number '1' in red was applied at some point on both sides of the nose to denote that aircraft's status as the first '*Serienflugzeuge*'.

3
Me 262A-1a Wk-Nr 170067 'White 3' of *E.Kdo* 262, Lechfeld, Germany, summer 1944
Most aircraft of *E.Kdo* 262 carried a yellow identification band, approximately 150 mm wide, on their fuselages aft of the cockpit and forward of the *Balkenkreuz*. The aircraft were also marked with their individual numbers as large white numerals on the nose, and early machines had their *Werknummern* in visibly large numerals below the tail *Hakenkreuz*.

4
Me 262A-1a 'White 1' of *Kdo. Nowotny*, Achmer, Germany, autumn 1944
The aircraft of *Kdo. Nowotny* were broadly similar in appearance to the machines of *E.Kdo* 262, although their uppersurfaces had areas of RLM 81 (*dunkelbraun*) and RLM 82 (*oliv grün*), with the base of the tail and the lower engine cowling surfaces in RLM 76 (*lichtblau*). The tail fins carried a characteristic blotch and scribble pattern. 'White 1' was assigned as a training machine and carried a white 'S' for '*Schulflugzeug*' on its rear fuselage.

5
Me 262A-1a 'White 7' of Oberfeldwebel Hermann Buchner, *Kdo. Nowotny*, Lechfeld, Germany, October 1944
'White 7' was finished in the typical colours of *Kdo. Nowotny*. Virtually all of the unit's jets carried their tactical numbers in white forward of the cockpit and had a yellow band applied to the fuselage forward of the *Balkenkreuz*. The fuselage itself has been finished in two shades of green, possibly RLM 82/83 (*dunkelgrün*). A number of *Kdo. Nowotny*'s Me 262s had the so-called 'tadpole'-marked tailplanes as delivered sub-assembly units, but it would appear this aircraft did not, retaining a more common late-war mottling.

6
Me 262A-1a Wk-Nr 130179 Black 'F' of *Kdo. Schenck*, Lechfeld, July 1944
Built at Schwäbisch-Hall, this aircraft was one of the first Me 262s delivered to *Kdo. Schenck* by Messerschmitt at Lechfeld in late June 1944. It is believed to have been flown by Schenck and Batel, the latter reporting several problems related to quality of build and functioning. The jet was destroyed in an air attack on 19 July 1944.

7
Me 262A-2a 9K+YH of 1./KG 51, Rheine, Germany, autumn 1944
Typical of Me 262s operating with I./KG 51 in late 1944, this aircraft was finished in a scribble pattern of greens RLM 80/82 with RLM 76 pale blue undersides. The tips to the nose and tail fin were in the *Staffel* colour of white.

8
Me 262A-1a 'Green 1' of Major Rudolf Sinner, *Stab* III./JG 7, Brandenburg-Briest, Germany, January 1945
Sinner's 'second' Me 262 as *Kommandeur* of III./JG 7 featured a pattern in 'reverse' to that of his first aircraft. This machine was finished in a diagonally striped pattern of RLM 82/83 bands running, from the port side, left to right along the fuselage. The individual markings appear to be identical to his first Me 262, with the aircraft's tactical number '1' in green immediately below the *Geschwader* emblem, the double chevron marking of a *Gruppenkommandeur*'s aircraft, the blue and red defence of the Reich identification band superimposed with the vertical bar of III. *Gruppe* and with a *Hakenkreuz* in solid white.

9
Me 262 A-1a Wk-Nr 111588 'White 5' of 11./JG 7, Brandenburg-Briest, Germany, January 1945
This Leipheim-built III. *Gruppe* Me 262 appears to have worn a late-war segmented uppersurface finish of RLM 81/83, with a high demarcation line along the RLM 76 fuselage sides over which a light mottle of these two uppersurface colours was applied. The aircraft's tactical number is in white, but it does not carry the *Geschwader* emblem of JG 7. The *Werknummer* has been stencilled in a standard location on the tailplane beneath the *Hakenkreuz*, but there are some unusual markings on the tail assembly and rudder – a vertical chevron and the number '17'. These may have been factory-applied part reference stencils.

10
Me 262A-2a Wk-Nr 170064 9K+BK of 2./KG 51, Rheine, Germany, October 1944
Believed to have been Leipheim-built Wk-Nr 170064, this aircraft was finished in a scribble pattern of RLM 80/82 greens with RLM 76 pale blue on its undersides. The 2. *Staffel* colour of red was used for the individual aircraft code, as well as the nose tip. This aircraft was possibly flown by Leutnant Hans Heid.

11
Me 262A-1a/U3 Wk-Nr 500259 'White 3' of 1./NAG 6, Eger or Lechfeld, Germany, March 1945
Built at Regensburg, this aircraft was converted into an A-1a/U3 at Eger and flight-tested by Flugkapitän Oeller on 19 March 1945. Transferred to 1./NAG 6 and flown by Unteroffizier Heinz Huxold, it appears to be finished in a blend of RLM 71 dark green with RLM 77 dark grey.

12
Me 262A-1a Wk-Nr 110556 'Red S' of JV 44, Brandenburg-Briest and Munich-Riem, Germany, March–April 1945
Built at Schwäbisch-Hall and believed to be one of the first aircraft on strength with JV 44, this aircraft was used for training rather than for operations, and it is known to have been flown by Oberfeldwebels Josef Dobnig and Rudolf Nielinger – the

first Me 262 each of these pilots flew. It has been finished in a splintered upper surface camouflage of RLM 81/82 that extends as a mottle over the fuselage, with a base of RLM 76. The red 'S' is somewhat thin in style, and an unusual stencilled 'A4' appears twice on the forward fuselage/nose and on the outboard side of the Jumo engine unit in three places. The meaning of this stencilling is not known.

13
Me 262A-1a Wk-Nr 111745 'White 5' of JV 44, Munich-Riem, Germany, April 1945

Built at the Kuno AG *Werk* 1 at Scheppach (Burgau), this aircraft is known to have been flown by Unteroffizieren Eduard Schallmoser and Karl-Heinz Müller. 'White 5' was very representative of JV 44's core aircraft – the batch of Me 262s used by the unit when it first arrived at Munich-Riem. The jet was finished in overall RLM 82 and featured only a white '5' – its tactical number – to distinguish it from other similarly finished machines. Its *Werknummer* was stencilled in black beneath the *Hakenkreuz*.

14
Me 262A-2a Wk-Nr 111685 'White F' of 1./KG 51, Hopsten, Germany, March 1945

Built at Schwäbisch-Hall, this aircraft displays typical late-war colours and white 1. *Staffel* markings. Delivered to 1./KG 51 at Hopsten on 15 March 1945, it then went to Memmingen and, finally, to München-Riem, where it was assigned to JV 44. The jet was found abandoned at the side of an Autobahn at war's end.

15
Me 262A-1 Wk-Nr 111620 'B3+GR' of 7./KG(J) 54, Neuburg/Donau, Germany, February 1945

This Leipheim-built aircraft was finished in a base coat of RLM 76, with heavy mottling of RLM 80/81 on the upper fuselage and nose. The 'G' and 'R' of the code were in white and black, respectively, while the *Werknummer* was applied in thin, stencilled numerals below the *Hakenkreuz*.

16
Me 262B-1a Wk-Nr 111643 'B3+ZM' of 4./KG(J) 54, Czechoslovakia, May 1945

This very used aircraft was found shortly after VE Day in a damaged state following a forced landing in Czechoslovakia, with the area of the fuselage bearing the unit code having been crudely cut away. It is possible the aircraft was passed to KG(J) 54 from KG 51, and it is shown here in the markings of the latter unit. The fuselage was finished in a dense mottle of RLM 81/82 over a base of RLM 76. The entire nose was a replacement unit finished in an RLM 02 (*grau*) primer, while the nose tip had crude filler lines which were greyish-yellow in colour. The engine intake ring was bare metal. The code was 'B3' in black, with the 'Z' in white and the 'M' also in black – another line of filler obscured part of the 'M'.

17
Me 262B-1a/U1 Wk-Nr 110305 'Red 8' of 10./NJG 11, Schleswig-Jagel, Germany, May 1945

The fuselage of this nightfighter was finished in a base coat of RLM 76, over which a very dense and heavy mottling of RLM 75 was applied. The tops of the engine units and wing uppersurfaces were probably RLM 83, with the lower areas of the engines and wing undersurfaces in black. The fuselage *Balkenkreuz* was a black outline and the aircraft's relatively small number '8' was applied in red, outlined in white, on the nose. The last three digits of the *Werknummer* were painted in white in a stencilled style on the tip of the nose.

18
Me 262B-1a/U1 Wk-Nr 110635 'Red 10' of 10./NJG 11, Schleswig-Jagel, Germany, May 1945

Like 'Red 8', this Me 262 nightfighter was finished in an overall base of RLM 76, with RLM 75 mottling on its uppersurfaces, fuselage sides and engine cowling tops. The undersurfaces (fuselage and wings) were in black, which extended up to the halfway point of the engine cowlings. The twin drop tanks were in the camouflage scheme as the aircraft's uppersurfaces.

19
Me 262A-1a 'B3+CR' of III./KG(J) 54, Neuburg/Donau, Germany, March 1945

This profile is based on photographs taken at Neuburg of such a machine assigned to III. *Gruppe*, although its fuselage code cannot be seen. The aircraft was finished in an overall green base colour, probably RLM 82, with a random scribble pattern applied over it, possibly RLM 77, which also extended over the top of the Jumo engine cowlings. This was not applied over the fuselage *Balkenkreuz*, but it did partially obscure the *Hakenkreuz*. The aircraft is depicted here with the code B3+CR of 7. *Staffel*.

20
Me 262A-1a/U3 Wk-Nr 500853 '29' probably of 1./NAG 6, Lechfeld, Germany, May 1945

Built in Obertraubling, this reconnaissance aircraft was found abandoned by Allied forces at Lechfeld. Its scribble pattern was probably formed of RLM 81/82 over RLM 77.

21
Me 262A-1a 'Green 2' of the *Geschwaderstab* JG 7, Brandenburg-Briest, Germany, April 1945

True to JG 7's tendency to experiment with camouflage schemes, this Me 262 is finished in a very non-standard 'tortoise shell' effect. It is possible that this was applied in RLM 83 over a base of RLM 76. The tactical number, below the running fox *Geschwader* insignia, was probably in green, while the blue and red Reich air defence fuselage band appears to be absent. The aircraft carried a single chevron and extended horizontal bars on either side of the *Balkenkreuz*, denoting that the Me 262 was possibly assigned to the *Geschwader* Operations Officer or perhaps that it was another machine assigned to the *Kommodore*, Major Theodor Weissenberger. The *Hakenkreuz* was probably finished in solid white.

22
Me 262A-1a 'White 22' of JV 44, Munich-Riem and Salzburg-Maxglan, Germany, April 1945

Like 'White 5', this Me 262 was probably another of JV 44's early aircraft, and it was finished in RLM 82, but with possible areas of RLM 80. The tactical number, '22', was applied in an unusual squared-off style, and the aircraft was fitted with a replacement rudder.

23
Me 262A-1a 'Black 4' of JG 7, Prague-Rusin, Czechoslovakia, May 1945

The most distinguishing feature of 'Black 4' was its replacement nose section left in a light blue or grey primer. Its tactical number, which was outlined in white, was of the 'closed' variety, and it had the blue and red defence of the Reich fuselage band of JG 7 aft of the *Balkenkreuz*. Unless the *Geschwader* emblem had been applied to the original nose section, then it appears none was ever added to this jet in the standard location.

24
Me 262A-2a Wk-Nr 111712 of JV 44, Munich-Riem and
Innsbruck-Hötting, Germany, April–May 1945
This aircraft was devoid of any colouring except for its engine units, which were sprayed RLM 76, with RLM 81 over the tops and sides. A replacement rudder was also fitted which, again, was finished in RLM 81. The aircraft was given a black-bordered fuselage cross, and the last three digits of its *Werknummer* were applied to the very rear fuselage and in the area between the *Hakenkreuz* and above the horizontal stabiliser. While the tail unit was coated with primer, the rest of the aircraft had been left in bare metal, with the fuselage panel joints showing filler paste. As an Me 262A-2a, the aircraft would have been fitted with bomb racks (as depicted here), and there was also head armour for the pilot.

SELECTED BIBLIOGRAPHY AND SOURCES

Unpublished Sources

Interview transcript Walter Hagenah, June 1976 (via Boyne)
Interview transcript Karl Schnörrer, October 1978 (via Boyne)
Interview transcript Walter Windisch, 1976 (via Boyne)
'My time with the Me 262', private recollections by Herbert Schlüter
Correspondence with Hermann Buchner and Herbert Schlüter
Flugbuch – Oberleutnant Hans Peter Waldmann and Fahnenjunker-Feldwebel Heinrich Janssen
JG 7 Development – chart prepared by Manfred Griehl (author collection)
'The Me 262 as a Combat Aircraft', ADI(K) Report No 323/1945, 4 June 1945
Luftwaffenkommando West and AOC Norway and Italy – morning and evening situation reports, February–April 1945
'Zugang auc Inductrio' Stand 31/3/45 and 10/4/45 (prepared for OKL *Führungsstab*)
AIR20/7708 The Western Front 1–14 February 1945 – daily situation reports issued by OKL Operations Staff Ia, AHB6 translation No VII/130, April 1954
AIR20/7708 The Western Front 15–28 February 1945 – Daily situation reports issued by OKL Operations Staff Ia, AHB6 translation No VII/131, April 1954
AIR20/7709 AHB6 Translation No VII/137 Fighter Staff conferences 1944, June 1954
AIR22/418 Eighth and Fifteenth Air Force USAAF – weekly intelligence summaries Nos 52–82 1944, November 1945
AIR40/2377 HQ 2nd TAF, signal intelligence survey of GAF [German Air Force] activity – month of February 1945, March 1945
DEFE5 504/505/562/565/566/567/568/569/571/572/601 Ultra decrypts
HW5/685 reports of German Army and Air Force high grade machine decrypts, Apr 1–Apr 2, 1945/686, Apr 3–Apr 4, 1945/688 and Apr 7–Apr 8, 1945

Selected Articles

Beale, Nick, I./NAG 1 and the Me 262 – January–April 1945 at www.ghostbombers.com
Beale, Nick, *Einsatzkommando* KG 51 – 24–31 August 1944 at www.ghostbombers.com
Haefner, Heinrich, 'Die letzten Einsätze der deutschen Luftwaffe mit der Messerschmitt Me 262 vom 1', Januar-8 Mai 1945, *Luftwaffen-Revue* 2/98
Steinhoff, Johannes, 'The Weapon that Nearly Succeeded', *RAF Flying Review* Vol 9 No 5, February 1954

Books

Boehme, Manfred, *JG 7 – The World's First Jet Fighter Unit 1944/1945*, Schiffer Military History, 1992
Boehme, Manfred, *Strahlaufklärer Messerschmitt Me 262 – Die Geschichte der Nahaufklärungsgruppe 6*, VDM Heinz Nickel, 2000
Boiten, Dr Theo and Mackenzie, Roderick J, *Nachtjagd War Diaries – An Operational History of the German Night Fighter Force in the West Volume Two April 1944–May 1945*, Red Kite, 2008
Brown, David, Janda, Ales, Poruba, Tomas and Vladar, Jan, *Messerschmitt Me 262s of KG & KG(J) units*, JaPo, 2010
Budiansky, Stephen, *Air Power – From Kitty Hawk to Gulf War II: A History of the People, Ideas and Machines that Transformed War in the Century of Flight*, Viking, 2003
Buttler, Tony, *Osprey X-Planes 11 – Jet Prototypes of World War II*, Osprey Publishing, 2019
Hallion, Richard P, *Taking Flight – Inventing the Aerial Age From Antiquity Through the First World War*, Oxford University Press Inc, 2003
Horn, Jan, *Das Flurschaden-Geschwader – Die Chronik des Kampfgeschwaders 51 "Edelweiß" zwischen dem 1. Januar 1944 bis Kriegsende*, Jan Horn, 2010
O'Connell, Dan, *Messerschmitt Me 262 – The Production Log 1941–1945*, Classic Publications, 2005
Radtke, Siegfried, *Kampfgeschwader 54 – Von der Ju 52 zur Me 262: Eine Chronik nach Kriegstagebüchern, Dokumenten und Berichten 1935–1945*, Schild Verlag, 1990
Schmoll, Peter, *Nest of Eagles – Messerschmitt Production and Flight-Testing at Regensburg 1936–1945*, Classic Publications, 2009
Sharp, Dan, *Messerschmitt Me 262 – Development & Politics*, Tempest Books, 2022
Smith, J Richard and Creek, Eddie J, *Me 262 Volume Ones to Four*, Classic Publications, 1997, 1998 and 2000
Steinhoff, Johannes, *The Last Chance – The Pilots' Plot Against Göring*, Hutchinson, 1977
Zapf, Andreas, *The Jet Night Fighters – Kurt Welter and the story of the Messerschmitt Me 262 Night Fighters*, self-published, undated

INDEX